Communication Skills
FOR
DUMMIES®

by Elizabeth Kuhnke

WILEY

A John Wiley and Sons, Ltd, Publication

Communication Skills For Dummies®

Published by:
John Wiley & Sons, Ltd
The Atrium
Southern Gate
Chichester
West Sussex
PO19 8SQ
England
www.wiley.com

Registered office

John Wiley & Sons Ltd, The Atrium, Southern Gate, Chichester, West Sussex, PO19 8SQ, United Kingdom

For details of our global editorial offices, for customer services and for information about how to apply for permission to reuse the copyright material in this book please see our website at www.wiley.com.

For general information on our other products and services, please contact our Customer Care Department within the U.S. at 877-762-2974, outside the U.S. at (001) 317-572-3993, or fax 317-572-4002. For technical support, please visit www.wiley.com/techsupport.

A catalogue record for this book is available from the British Library.

ISBN 978-1-118-40124-8 (pbk), ISBN 978-1-118-40126-2 (ebk),
ISBN 978-1-118-40127-9 (ebk), ISBN 978-1-118-40125-5 (ebk)

SKY10066594_020724

WILEY

Contents at a Glance

Table of Contents

Introduction

● ●

*M*ake no mistake: your ability to communicate with clarity, courage and commitment is your number one key to success at work and in your personal life. No matter how innovative your ideas, how sincere your feelings or how passionate your beliefs, if you fail to connect with other people and communicate in a way that persuades, inspires or motivates them, your efforts are going to be in vain.

You're never not communicating. Whether you're in a deep sleep, in a heated debate with a colleague or in a text-a-thon with a friend, in today's world of 24/7 communication you're always sending and receiving messages. Some people are outstanding communicators, listening for understanding in addition to conveying their own clear intentions, whereas others struggle to connect with their own message as well as with other people.

Great communication leads to understanding, intimacy and mutual appreciation. The good news is that you can develop and successfully apply communication skills, as long as you're willing to commit to the process and practise. As my father used to say, communication works for those who work at it.

If you want to be recognised as a committed and effective communicator, you need to concentrate and absorb the messages that people convey to you. As well as noticing the spoken words themselves, pay attention to the way the words are delivered. For example, does the speaker's voice rise at the end of a statement, making it sound like a question? Is the voice soft and difficult to hear? Are the spoken words straightforward and direct, or do they convey uncertainty and doubt? How the message is conveyed contains the core of the message.

When you're delivering a message, make sure that your intention is clear and your delivery is congruent with your message. Your aim is to connect with the people you're engaging with in order to achieve mutually satisfying goals and objectives.

About This Book

As an American, married to a German, living in England and working with multicultural teams and individuals around the globe, I'm very aware of the influence of culture – including gender, race and nationality – on communication. Although I devote one chapter specifically to communicating across cultures, my primary focus in this book is on Western communication practices. Writing this book, I've been selective in what I've chosen to include, with my aim being to offer you ways of communicating to enhance your personal and business relationships.

I explain how your attitude impacts on the content and delivery of your message. I describe how treating others with respect and establishing rapport increase your chances of creating clear and compelling communication. I show you how you can develop productive, profitable and positive relationships by listening with an open mind, being certain about the messages you want to convey and being prepared for challenging inter-actions. When you support the message you convey through words with body language – including gestures, expressions and posture, and voice – you increase your chances of com-municating successfully.

Whether you're writing your message, speaking face to face or using the various forms of communication technology, this book encourages you to listen to what others have to say, treat everyone with respect, maintain a clear intention about what you want to express and convey your message in a way the receiver can understand.

Conventions Used in This Book

Jargon can get in the way of clear communication and so I don't use any in this book. When I introduce a new term, I write it in *italics* and then define what it means. The only other conventions in this book are that web and email addresses are in monofont, and the action part of numbered steps and the key concepts in a list are in **bold**.

What You're Not to Read

The grey-tinted sidebars contain extra text, such as more detailed research information, that's not essential to understanding the section in question. By all means skip these boxes if you prefer, safe in the knowledge that you're not missing out on any essential tips or practical insights.

Foolish Assumptions

Although making assumptions can lead to misunderstandings, I set out mine here for clarity. In this book I assume that you:

- ✔ Are interested in communication skills and want to know a bit about the subject.

- ✔ Want to improve the way you communicate.

- ✔ Are willing to reflect on what you read and put into practice the suggestions I offer.

- ✔ Expect the best of yourself and others.

How This Book Is Organised

One of the coolest aspects about *For Dummies* books is that you can dip in and out as you please. You don't need to read Chapter 1 to understand what's coming next, and if you want to read the last chapter first, you can do so without ruining your enjoyment and missing out on any info. Whether you start at the end, jump into the middle or begin at the beginning, my hope is that you find what you're looking for. Turn to the table of contents or the index if you're in a rush to find out what you need. Otherwise, sit back, open the book wherever you want and enjoy the read. The following sections give you an idea of what to expect.

Part I: Honing Your Communication Skills

In Chapters 1 and 2, I explore the range of benefits to you of clear and respectful communication and the value of knowing what you want to achieve and how to go about attaining your desired outcomes. Chapter 3 covers some of the different personal communication preferences that you may encounter.

Part II: Being Receptive to Others

The thrust of this part is focusing on the person with whom you're communicating. In Chapters 4 and 5, you discover how building positive relationships and listening actively without barriers, such as prejudice and judgement, leads to successful communication.

Part III: Putting Your Mind and Body into Your Message

In this part you discover how your physical delivery in combination with your outlook can create clear, effective messages. I describe the impact of your attitude on communication (in Chapter 6) and how your voice (Chapter 7) and body language (Chapter 8) reflect your state of mind, perhaps unknowingly.

Part IV: Managing Communication Challenges

This part offers you insights and techniques for communicating with clarity and confidence whatever the difficulties. I cover navigating your way through awkward situations in Chapter 9 and negotiations in Chapter 10, where one wrong word can create havoc. I lead you through communicating successfully with people from cultures different from your own in Chapter 11.

Part V: Communicating Across Distances

In this part I help you uncover methods of communicating through technologies, ancient and bang up to date. Chapter 12 describes using social media and email, while Chapter 13 involves the slightly less novel form of the telephone! In addition, if you want to communicate in the traditional way with pen and paper, you find how to compose correspondence that's sure to impress in Chapter 14.

Part VI: The Part of Tens

If you're keen to cut to the core of communication quickly, begin with the two chapters in this part. Chapter 15 contains valuable hints on communicating in person and Chapter 16 is a concise overview of great communication skills.

Icons Used in This Book

For sharpening your thinking and focusing your attention, I use the following icons in the pages' margins:

This icon highlights relevant stories about family members, friends, clients, colleagues or just people I've observed. I hope they entertain and enlighten you about the joys and sorrows inherent in communication.

Here's a chance for you to view communication from a business perspective. By putting communication into a business context I help you see where you can keep doing what you're doing or perhaps make a few helpful changes.

This symbol underscores a valuable point to keep in mind.

This icon indicates practical and immediate remedies for honing your communication skills.

Here you can have a go at putting theory into practice. I've designed these exercises to enhance your skills and turn you into a first-rate communicator.

Everyone makes mistakes from time to time, but if you take note of the common errors that I place beside this icon you can steer clear of the worst. Other people have made these mistakes so that you don't need to!

Where to Go from Here

Each chapter of this book addresses a specific aspect of communication, from improving your listening skills to communicating efficiently through the written word, from appreciating different styles of communicating to establishing how to reach your communication goals.

Although I've designed all the information within these covers to support you in being a top-flight communicator, not everything is going to be pertinent to your specific requirements or interests. So you can read this book in any order that pleases you and in your own time: what, when and where you want.

If you're interested in writing an impressive business-related or personal letter, turn to Chapter 14, and to discover the important impact of your attitude on communication, have a look at Chapter 6. If communicating across cultures concerns you, flip to Chapter 11.

So kick off your shoes, sit back and prepare to pick up a few tips and techniques for becoming the superb communicator you deserve to be. I sincerely hope that you enjoy the journey and benefit from reading this book.

Part I
Honing Your Communication Skills

'I find Blenkinsop's powers of persuasive communication slightly worrying.'

In this part...

*T*his part sets you on the path to becoming an accomplished communicator. Here you can find out the essentials for connecting with your listener and building robust relationships. I show you how to present your case with clarity and conviction, and how to speak successfully with anyone at any time.

Chapter 1

Grasping the Finer Points of Great Communication

*Y*ou're always communicating. Whether you're dozing by the hearth on a chilly autumn night, praising your children for their successes at school or admonishing an employee for showing up late for work – again – you're continuously sending out messages through your words, voice and body.

Sometimes your communications are crystal clear, such as when your eyes are sparkling, your mouth is in a full-blown smile and you're holding your arms out wide ready to embrace a returning loved one. But at other times you can convey an unintended message, such as appearing sad, angry or despondent when in fact you're simply considering how to respond to a challenging situation. As a result, taking a level of control about how and what you communicate is vitally important in your personal and business lives.

In this chapter you discover the fundamental points for communicating like a pro, which involves using more than just your mouth and the words you say. I guide you through preparing yourself mentally for conveying your messages clearly and connecting with others who have different points of view from yours. You also have a quick glance into the value of treating other people with respect and taking the time to listen to what someone else has to say before coming in with your opinion. In addition, I provide a series of steps for handling difficult situations.

Using Your Whole Body to Communicate

Great communicators aim to understand others before making themselves understood. They grasp not only what people are saying through their spoken words, but also recognise what others (and themselves) convey through body language, emotional responses and vocal quality.

If you take one message from this book (and I hope you find many, many more!), remember that conveying information involves all aspects of your personality, your mind, your eyes and ears as well as your mouth and facial expressions, and how you stand, gesture and move your entire body.

Getting into the right frame of mind

By getting into the right frame of mind I mean ensuring that you have a good attitude, and so let go of negative thoughts and beliefs that serve as barriers to accomplished communication. Ditch judgement and blame and think about how you want the conversation to proceed. (In Chapter 6 you find suggestions for checking your attitude.)

Negative thoughts and beliefs that may hamper communication include:

- ✔ Finding fault with the other person

- ✔ Disparaging other people's ideas

- ✔ Belittling individuals' beliefs

- ✔ Ridiculing someone else's point of view

Knowing what you want to achieve and being open to hearing what the other person has to say are the foundations for great communication. If the old saying 'energy follows thought' is true, whatever you focus on achieving in a conversation is what you can achieve.

When you approach communication free of murky thoughts, you can let your linguistic wizardry steer you towards free and open relationships.

Entering a dialogue with an optimistic focus heightens your chances of communicating successfully.

Putting your eyes and ears to work

The best communicators have a keen sense of observation, paying attention to what they see and hear, keeping their perception antennae tuned and registering what they observe. They gauge accurately their surroundings and people's behaviour, noting the mundane, the extraordinary and points in between.

Here are some suggestions for improving your observational skills:

- ✔ **Make eye contact with people you see, whether you know them or not, and observe how they respond.** If they look back at you, they're signalling that they noticed you and are observing in return. Be careful not to stare, however, because your interest may be misinterpreted by the other person.

- ✔ **Watch how people move their bodies.** You can tell if people are willing to engage with you – or not – by the way they move in your direction or pull away. Observe whether people are lethargic or energetic. Listen for the words they use and the pitch, pace and tone of their voices. These telltale signs often reveal more about people than what they say about themselves.

- ✔ **Open your peripheral vision and take in a panoramic view of your surroundings.** Let your brain receive and release ordinary things, to avoid excess analysis.

✔ **Eliminate distractions when you're at work or interacting with others.** Putting away your electronic devices
when you're with others enables you to notice what's
going on around you and so engage in more effective
communication.

Communicating with Clarity

Take a moment and consider just how often you communicate
with people throughout your day and the importance of getting
across your messages accurately:

✔ You write emails and use social media (the subject of
Chapter 12).

✔ You speak on the phone (check out Chapter 13).

✔ You compose formal letters (which I discuss in Chapter 14).

✔ You participate in face-to-face meetings and debates with
friends and colleagues (for a collection of essential hints,
see Chapter 15).

Your cave-dwelling ancestors only had to grunt, smile and
frown to make themselves understood! (Which reminds me,
to discover ways of physically speaking more clearly, turn to
Chapter 7.) Today, the expanding forms and nature of communication put the burden on you to be clear about what
you want and then communicate in a candid way so that your
aims are clearly understood.

Sending a clear message

If you've ever sat through a meeting, presentation or even
a dinner-party conversation thinking, 'What's this person
talking about?,' 'What's the message here?' you're not alone.
Without exception, every one of my clients shares tales of
sitting through confusing meetings and presentations that
are time-wasting experiences.

To send a clear message you need a clear, concise idea of what
you want to accomplish (as I describe in the later section
'Being clear about your goals, needs and preferences').

Although this 'core idea' is what you want your listener to remember, you then need to back it up with lucid suggestions and unambiguous, structured and logical recommendations that your listener can grasp. In addition, you have to persuade others to buy into your message. Getting people to invest personally in your idea requires a bit more thought.

 The next time you're sending a message to your team, boss or any stakeholder, create a story that provides both a logical and an emotional rationale for people to come on-board. This approach is an essential way to gain buy-in, because you're ringing the bells of people who, like you, can benefit from your ideas and recommendations. People tend to buy on feelings and justify with facts, so by appealing to both their emotions and their intellect, you're onto a winner.

As you're planning your message, think about your audience and what the individuals care about most. Make sure that you include the type of information expected by the other person, which for some may be facts and hard data while others prefer subjective opinions and feelings... Crunch the numbers, gather your facts and analyse how your findings support the core idea. Ensure that you supply only the necessary information to avoid boring or confusing your listeners. By sending a clear, concise and well-substantiated message, you stand a good chance of having your ideas accepted and acted upon.

In Chapter 2 you can find lots of tips for sending clear messages.

Providing feedback

As part of making sure that you're understood at work, and in order to enhance people's growth and development and improve their performance at work or at home, provide them with feedback. Given correctly, feedback can improve morale, avoid dispiriting misunderstandings and reduce confusion around expectations and performance.

 Appropriate feedback can help others improve the quality of their work and boost your interpersonal relationships with your employees.

Feedback: it's rocket science!

The German philosopher and psychologist Kurt Lewin (1890–1947) was one of the early proponents of group dynamics and action research directed towards solving social problems. Lewin pioneered the practice of T-group training, in which participants find out about themselves through feedback, problem-solving procedures and role play. The technique was first designed as a means of changing attitudes, beliefs and behaviours of individuals. The practice of sharing emotions, as opposed to making judgements or drawing conclusions, enables people to understand how the way they speak and behave can produce specific emotional responses in others.

Lewin borrowed the term 'feedback' from electrical engineering and rocket science. When a rocket in space sends messages to Earth, mechanisms receive and interpret the signals and then send feedback to the rocket in order that it can correct its position or make repairs. Lewin compared humans to rockets, in that people send out signals through their words, body language, actions and other behaviours. When receivers catch the signals, they respond through feedback that's intended to adjust other people's behaviour.

You can provide two kinds of feedback:

- ✓ **Positive feedback:** To reinforce desired behaviour.
- ✓ **Constructive feedback:** To address areas that need improving.

Both forms of feedback are useful for improving and maintaining quality performance.

Providing positive feedback

The following steps and example statements are a guide for offering positive feedback:

1. **Describe the positive behaviour.** 'I thought you did a great job at the client meeting. You asked a lot of valuable, open-ended questions to understand the client's needs and concerns and expressed interest in the issues they're facing.'

2. **Explain why the behaviour is positive.** 'You treated the client with a lot of respect, and the way you built rapport through discovering similarities between you and them led to them opening up and offering us information we didn't have before. This added data can help us design a winning proposal.'

3. **Thank and encourage the individual.** 'I want to thank you for your efforts. As long as you continue approaching clients in this way you're going to have great success in this business.'

Giving constructive feedback

People frequently shy away from providing constructive feedback because they're concerned about upsetting the other person. That's not surprising because this type of feedback usually focuses on what people did wrong or could do better, instead of what they did well. If feedback is not constructive, the message won't be received or may even be perceived as an insult.

The difference between criticising and providing constructive feedback is in the intention and the way the feedback is delivered. Constructive feedback provides information about performance and behaviour based on objective standards. Delivered properly, recipients feel positive about themselves and their work. Criticism tends to be personal and subjective. For example, if you were to say, 'Your presentation was a mess. Your content was a jumble of unrelated points, impossible to follow and no one could hear what you were saying,' you would be criticising without offering any constructive comments. Instead you could say, 'You had a lot of information in your presentation, some of which was difficult to follow because the points seemed unrelated. In addition, your voice was hard to hear. The next time I suggest you structure your content in related groups, and practise in the room where you'll be presenting to make sure the people in the back row can hear you.' Constructive feedback aids the person receiving the information while criticising only points out what's wrong without offering concrete advice on how to improve.

The purpose of constructive feedback is to provide as clearly and accurately as possible:

- ✔ Encouragement
- ✔ Support
- ✔ Corrective measures
- ✔ Direction

The following guidelines help you provide constructive feedback at work, so that it has value for the recipient and for your organisation:

1. **State the purpose of your feedback.** Briefly say what you want to cover and the reasons why it's important. If you're initiating the feedback, explain that you'd like to offer some feedback and make sure the feedback topic means that the recipient doesn't have to guess what you want to talk about. If the other person has asked you to provide feedback, a focusing statement makes sure that you're addressing the expressed need. You can start off the feedback session with statements such as:

   - 'I'm concerned about. . .'.
   - 'You need to know that. . .'.
   - 'I want to discuss. . .'.
   - 'I have some concerns about. . .'.
   - 'I noticed that when you. . .'.
   - 'I was pleased to observe that you. . .'.

   Feedback is frequently offered to help improve performance, but it's also useful for reinforcing positive behaviour.

2. **Relate what you specifically observed.** Have in mind a certain event or behaviour that you can address, including when and where it happened, who was involved and what resulted. Stick to your own personal observations and don't speak for others. Avoid generalities such as 'always', 'usually' and 'never'. For example, perhaps say, 'At yesterday's marketing meeting I noticed that you raised your voice when you were speaking to Robert.'

3. **Describe your reactions.** Tell the other person what consequences they can expect as a result of their behaviour and how you feel about it. Give examples of how the actions affected you and others, such as 'The support team looked embarrassed and I felt uncomfortable when you shouted and denigrated their efforts. Name-calling and shouting are unacceptable behaviour in this office.'

   By describing your reactions to the behaviour and the potential consequences, people understand how their behaviour impacts on individuals and the organisation.

4. **Allow the other person to respond.** After you've spoken, remain silent and look the person in the eye. This behaviour indicates that you're waiting for a response. If the other person remains silent you can elicit a response by asking an open-ended question such as:

   • 'What do you think?'

   • 'How do you view this situation?'

   • 'What's your reaction to my comments?'

   • 'Tell me your thoughts about this.'

5. **Provide specific suggestions.** Offer practical, viable and reasonable examples that can help people improve their performance. When you give suggestions you're showing that you've moved on from your evaluations and are looking to improve the situation. No matter how well people are performing, they can benefit from further ideas to do even better.

   Only offer an idea, however, if you think the other person is going to benefit and find it useful. For example, you can say, 'Kelly, rather than telling Michael that you're not interested in the details of his proposal, you can ask him about his ideas that most interest you.'

6. **Summarise and express your support.** Go over the major points you discussed and summarise the action items to lead to improved performance. Focus on what the other person can do differently in the future and finish up on a positive, encouraging note by expressing your confidence in the person's ability to improve the situation. For example, 'As I said, the group looks up to you and feels confused and upset when you speak

to them harshly. I know that you want to create a positive atmosphere among the new members of staff and I have confidence in your ability to create a happy and productive environment.'

By summarising, you can check that your communication is clear and avoid misunderstandings. In addition, by showing your support at the end of the feedback session you finish on a positive note.

Being clear about your goals, needs and preferences

If your goals are uncertain and have a tendency to change, you can't expect others to understand what you're trying to communicate. After all, trying to nail down the moving target of ever-changing goals and expectations is a worthless exercise. Also, when you're unsure about what you want to accomplish, how can you expect to convey a clear message to others? Clear goals are crucial if you, your clients and your colleagues are to communicate successfully.

In any relationship, whether at home or at work, letting others know your needs and preferences is vital if you want them met. Instead of hiding what you really want, and waiting for others to come up with the correct guess, owning up to what works for you saves time and clarifies communication. Stating your needs and preferences in a non-threatening way enhances communication by clarifying expectations.

Frequently, you hear people say, 'Oh, I don't care,' 'Whatever you want' or 'You decide,' leaving the decision-making responsibility on the shoulders of the other person. But other people can end up making decisions that work for them and aren't what you want at all. Instead, articulate what you need and what your preferences are so that you create your own satisfying result.

Failing to speak out and asking for what you want can lead to strife and resentment. To avoid feeling deprived, disappointed and dissatisfied, express your needs and preferences clearly, knowing that you have the right and responsibility to speak up for what you want.

Chapter 2 addresses the importance of knowing what you're communicating and provides hints and tips for conveying your needs and preferences.

Some cultures discourage open expression of personal preferences. Check out Chapter 11 for more about communicating with people from different cultures.

Distinguishing between personal and business conversations

Essential to communicating with clarity is knowing the type of communication you're involved in and acting appropriately. If you employ an unsuitable approach, you give off mixed signals, creating confusion and possibly offence.

Personal and business communication is different in several ways, including form, content and purpose. In personal conversations you can afford – and are expected – to be informal, casual and relaxed, adjusting your tone of voice depending on whether you're speaking to a child, a friend or an aged relative. In business conversations you're focused on a subject that has professional implications, requiring a more formal tone and wording as you seek to further your career goals.

Although you may use slang and even be a bit crude when talking to a friend, you're looked upon with suspicion if you speak that way against the formal backdrop of an office environment. When you enquire about a client's golf game, a customer's child or a colleague's ailing parent, you're demonstrating a polite interest without crossing into personal territory.

The simple rule for business conversations is to keep the tone professional and the purpose clear. Of course you can speak with trusted colleagues or business relations in a casual manner as long as the conversation is appropriate for the environment.

Displaying Respect for Other People

Effective communication requires the people involved to trust one another, which means that respect is needed on both sides. Listening with the intention to understand, appreciating other people's opinions and making efforts to detect and adopt others' communication preferences are all part of showing respect.

Behaving respectfully

Being aware of the impact of your actions on other people and recognising the fundamental worth of individuals is at the heart of behaving respectfully. If you keep in mind the rule 'treat others as they want to be treated', you're well set to treat people with respect.

Behaving respectfully doesn't mean that you have to like or agree with the person, organisation or institution you're engaging with. Instead, you have to bring integrity, honesty and truthfulness to all your relationships, including, but not limited to:

- ✔ Valuing the opinions of others.
- ✔ Listening to others before expressing your point of view.
- ✔ Appreciating people's privacy.
- ✔ Treating people with kindness, courtesy and politeness.
- ✔ Never insulting, name-calling or disparaging people or their ideas.
- ✔ Never belittling, demeaning or patronising others.
- ✔ Treating people consistently and fairly.
- ✔ Praising more frequently than you criticise.

If you want others to respect you, you have to respect them.

Turn to Chapter 5 for the benefits of treating people with respect.

Listening with an open mind

Listening properly is fundamental to communication and behaving with respect, and it's an active exercise rather than something that just happens. Good listeners concentrate and put effort into understanding the spoken words and underlying feelings that individuals are communicating. Listening with an open mind means focusing on the person speaking and closing the door on prejudice, preconceptions and assumptions.

When you listen with an open mind you're willing to be influenced by what you hear and consider the merit in what someone else is saying. Self-discipline is an essential element of listening with an open mind because it stops you from anticipating what your conversational partner is going to say and jumping to conclusions, a common behaviour. When you do so before hearing the other person out, you're bound to find yourself in a mire of misunderstanding.

The hardest time to listen with an open mind is when you're receiving a message you don't want to hear; for example, when your boss is debriefing you on your behaviour at a client meeting where you contradicted the agreed approach. Here's when you have to muster up all your reserves of self-control to avoid pushing back against a message that makes you want to squirm with shame, anger, embarrassment and any other uncomfortable feelings you can think of. Although listening with an open mind can sometimes be tough and testing, doing so is worth the effort.

I list a few barriers to open-minded listening below with some examples to help clarify. You may notice that many are inter-related and more than one can happen at the same time:

✓ **Judgemental listening:** The receiver listens with the intention of determining whether the speaker is right or wrong.

Nigel is talking about problems he's having with one of his valued employees. He admits that he fired the guy without having anyone to replace him. Nigel's wife, Ros judges him and thinks to herself, 'Well, that was a stupid thing to do.' By judging Nigel's behaviour, she's closing herself off from listening to his feelings and concerns.

✔ **Distorted listening:** Here the receiver listens through filters, such as personal prejudices, that distort what the speaker is saying.

Andrea is talking about her new friend, Lynne, who's a lesbian. One of Andrea's work colleagues, Al, has a distorted image of 'those kinds of people' and thinks 'If she's hanging out with her, she's setting herself up for big trouble.' What Al fails to hear are all the good things Andrea has been saying about Lynne.

✔ **Stereotype-based listening:** The listener has built-in prejudices that get in the way of receiving the message.

John, head of a global team of engineers, is speaking with Maria, one of the clerical workers on the project. Maria makes some insightful observations, which Nigel fails to hear because he thinks of her as 'just a clerk'.

✔ **Resistive listening:** Some people have an immediate aversion to ideas that aren't their own. They can also be so conservative in their views that they see anything that challenges their thinking as the enemy.

Fiona is a member of the church choir. When the new choirmaster proposes that the choir include some modern hymns in their repertoire, Fiona thinks to herself, 'Why can't people just leave things as they are?'.

✔ **Interpretive listening:** In this instance, people use their own life experiences and beliefs to interpret rather than understand what the other is saying.

Henry is talking about the problems he's having with his father. His friend Susan, a big fan of Freudian psychology, laughs and says, 'Ah, another case of the Oedipus complex. Why don't you stop competing with your father for your mother's affections and get on with your life?' Her filter of psychological theory colours her hearing.

✔ **Past-behaviour-based listening:** Here listening is based on a person's past experiences of the speaker, not allowing for the possibility of change.

From Seb's experiences of Angie during the time he's known her, he expects her to complain about everything. Even when she's doing her best to change this behaviour, he hears her complaining no matter what she says.

✔ **Attraction-based listening:** The receiver connects the truth of what someone says to how attractive – or not – the receiver finds the speaker.

Emma thinks George is attractive and whatever he says sounds good to her. She finds David unappealing and so his opinions always sound foolish.

Open-minded listening avoids these traps as much as possible. I say 'as much as possible' because even the best-intended people are influenced by the various cultures that colour their lives (such as family, country, religion and so on). These cultures spawn *filters,* or ways of seeing the world, that inform beliefs, opinions and points of view. The most accomplished communicators accept that they grow up with filters, but still do their best to concentrate on what other people are actually saying.

Open-minded listening isn't the same as approving of what the other person is saying. For example, when I listen to my friend Rick's ideas about politics I seldom approve of his point of view. I do, however, aim to listen with an open mind with the intention of finding out something I hadn't considered before.

For more tips on remaining responsive to new ideas and using open-ended questions, as well as other essentials on communicating effectively, go to Chapter 16.

Connecting with different types of people

No two people are exactly alike. Although some are more similar to you than others, everyone has their own unique way of seeing and making sense of the world (which is something you can exploit during negotiations, as I describe in Chapter 10). Your ability to connect with different types of people affects the quality of your communication and determines the success or failure of conveying messages and being understood.

In order to connect successfully with people who are different from you, you first need to want to connect. When you take the trouble to understand your own personality type and preferred method of communicating and discerning those of others, you bring a powerful dynamic to your relationships, allowing for better understanding and communication.

In Chapter 3 you gain insights into the benefit of engaging with people who are different from you.

Handling Challenging Communications

At some point in your life, if it hasn't happened already, you're going to come up against a situation filled with the potential for challenging communication. Whether you're facing a make-or-break interview, dealing with a disgruntled individual or ending a long-term relationship, you can make the best of a bad deal by being mentally prepared.

When you take the time to figure out what may be coming, you avoid the negative nervous energy that courses through your veins when you're unprepared. Dealing with people's difficult behaviour – whether they're your most valued client who's really angry with you or your best friend who's finding fault with the way you behave after one drink too many – requires you to take the following steps to smooth things over and leave the other person feeling satisfied:

1. **Fine-tune your way of thinking.** When you realise that someone is presenting you with a challenge, get into that person's mindset and point of view. Put aside any negative feelings about the situation or the other party and focus solely on them and their feelings about the situation.

2. **Listen actively.** Give people time to air their grievances and be heard. Perhaps say something along the lines of, 'Tell me what happened' or 'Tell me what's upsetting you.' By speaking this way you subtly form a partnership between you and the other person and indicate that you're ready and willing to listen. Avoid jumping to conclusions or trying to solve the problem. With this step you're aiming to encourage the other party to tell their story. (You can pick up more tips about active listening in Chapter 4.)

3. **Repeat the expressed concerns.** By clarifying your understanding you're sure to address the right issue. If you're uncertain, ask questions to identify the dif-

ficulty correctly. Make sure that your tone is calm and your language is objective. By rephrasing what's been said, you show that you've been listening and focusing on the situation that needs to be resolved.

4. **Demonstrate empathy.** Show through your words, tone of voice and body language that you care about how the other person feels. (You can find out how your body language can calm troubled waters, as well as how the way you use your voice can comfort listeners, in Chapter 8.)

5. **Offer a solution.** If you have an idea how to resolve the problem, let the other person know and then follow through. If you're not sure what's necessary to improve the situation, or if the other person resists your offer, ask for their suggestions. As long as you show willingness to resolve the problem, you stand a good chance of successfully addressing the challenge.

6. **Confirm what you're going to do and follow through.** When you've addressed the challenge, take immediate action (you can find ideas for managing tricky situations in Chapter 9). Aim to go above and beyond expectations to change a difficulty into a win– win result. (In Chapter 10, I offer you suggestions for handling challenging negotiations.)

7. **Learn from the feedback you receive.** Identify how the problem began and what made it escalate. By getting to the root of the problem and fixing it immediately, you may be able to avert challenging communications in the future. If you can't do that, at least you now have the skills for dealing with them.

If all else fails in a challenging situation, keep calm and carry on, practising the preceding steps.

Chapter 2

Knowing What You Want to Achieve

. . . .

In This Chapter

▶ Addressing what's important to you

▶ Considering your listener's needs

▶ Dealing with roadblocks that impede your success

. . . .

*1*f what you see every day in shops and cafes is representative, a lot of people need to work on their communication. Plenty of people appear to think that communication consists of talking at people and hoping that some of what they say sticks. You'd never guess that the purpose of communication is to convey clear messages that other people understand.

Often the problem is that speakers aren't clear even in their own minds of what they want to achieve, and so unsurprisingly they fail to communicate in a way that makes sense to those listening (see Chapter 4 for more about listening). Listeners misinterpret messages because these speakers fail to consider two points:

✔ What they want to happen as a result of delivering their message.

✔ How to deliver their message in a way that listeners can grasp.

In this chapter I show you how to create a purpose for communicating and take you through expressing your ideas in a clear, concise and concrete way. You discover how to create and convey a coherent, compelling, credible and complete message.

Communicating with a Clear Intention

The best communicators communicate with intention. They know what they want to accomplish and they're willing to do what they need to do in order to achieve their goals. Before they open their mouths they set themselves a purpose or plan, something to aim for. Having visualised a desired outcome, they communicate in ways that resonate with their listeners. (Chapter 4 explores how to listen for understanding, and Chapter 5 addresses connecting with listeners.)

When you know what you want to achieve and your message is focused and stated so that your listener can relate to it – rather than being confused or threatened – you can communicate with confidence and composure. With intention you gain control of your goals as well as your conversations. To quote Ralph Waldo Emerson, 'A good intention clothes itself with power.'

Here are some possible intentions that you may have when speaking:

- ✔ Establishing rapport

- ✔ Communicating respect

- ✔ Delivering value to enhance the lives of your clients, colleagues, friends or family members

- ✔ Changing a conflicting atmosphere into a co-operative one

- ✔ Overcoming your listeners' hesitancy to accept your ideas

- ✔ Offering reassurance

- ✔ Gaining information

- ✔ Selling an idea, concept or yourself

- ✔ Giving and receiving feedback

Your intention gives your communication direction and determines the outcome.

In this section I share some tips on speaking assertively, getting your meaning clear and committing to it: in other words, saying what you mean and meaning what you say.

Declaring your needs and preferences

In order to speak clearly and confidently, and with a clear intention, you can't shy away from speaking up for yourself, or be worried about putting your foot in your mouth, offending others or sounding like a stroppy old moo! Speaking assertively – that is, in a clear, open and reasonable way and not aggressively or passively – can improve your communication and your relationships. You leave no doubt in other people's minds when you clearly and calmly declare your needs and preferences.

When you state your position in a balanced and assertive manner, neither attacking others nor hiding your own beliefs, needs and feelings, you can feel confident that your intentions are clear, which is vital for helping you achieve your goals. In Chapter 6 I offer you specific guidelines and techniques for expressing your feelings.

If you find yourself struggling to communicate what's important to you because you're afraid of how others may respond, turn to your values (such as equality, honesty, perseverance, loyalty, reliability and so on). Your values are part of what make you the person you are and they direct your thoughts and actions.

Being certain about your values helps you communicate what's important to you with clarity and confidence.

Saying what you mean

Okay, confession time! I've been known to speak before being clear about what I mean and I expect that you've fallen victim to the habit from time to time as well. Although you have a vague intention, plan or idea in your mind, your message lacks focus and attention. As a result, when you speak your meaning is hard to follow.

Intentions are identified as two types:

> ✔ **Passive intentions:** These intentions are vague, indefinable and unfocused. When you're unclear about your intentions people can misinterpret what you mean or ignore what you say, leading to results you don't want.

✔ **Active intentions:** These intentions are clear and engaged. They're positive, move ideas forward and are more likely to give you the response you desire.

Passive intentions

Passive intentions can take the following forms:

✔ **A passing thought:** 'I wonder if. . .'.

✔ **Conflicting thoughts:** 'I could take this approach, but if I do then. . .'.

✔ **Vague ideas:** 'Maybe I should. . .'.

✔ **Uncommitted opinions:** 'Someday it may be nice to consider. . .'.

Some speakers prefer to remain in a state of indecision, allowing listeners to take responsibility for the words they hear. That way they can avoid being blamed for mistakes if things go wrong. Living in this type of passive state excuses them of all responsibility, but also means that they miss out on receiving the credit when things go right and don't always get what they want from life.

When you allow passive intentions to shape the way you communicate, your listeners struggle to understand what you mean and may ignore what you're trying to say.

Active intentions

Active intentions include the following:

✔ **A clearly visualised outcome:** 'I'm standing at the podium, feeling excited and motivated. I'm smiling, my mouth is moist and my stomach feels calm. The audience is on its feet applauding and cheering for more. . .'.

✔ **Committed thoughts:** 'I will turn in this project on Friday at 10 a.m. so that you can . . . in time for. . .'.

✔ **Robust, definite and detailed thoughts:** 'I will take the following three steps on Monday morning to gain approval from . . . so that we can. . .'.

✔ **Clear thoughts that give you a feeling of peace and satisfaction:** 'I will find a point of agreement, no matter how small; a common concern between you and me that. . .'.

If you've got something to say, say it. Don't make people guess what you're thinking and feeling. Guessing games are a fun diversion over the holidays, but they're ineffective for getting what you want. Unless, of course, your aim requires you to appear mysterious and enigmatic, in which case keep your thoughts and feelings to yourself.

Active intentions in action

Before speaking, think. Make sure that what you're saying is what you mean and what really matters to you, or else you may end up getting something you don't want.

To help you determine and say what you mean, make time in your day to create active intentions for what you want. When your intentions are clear and you're confident about what you want to say and how you're going to speak, state them out loud, both to yourself when you're on your own and to friends, family members and anyone else who'll listen to you. The more you articulate your thoughts, the clearer they become.

Although active intentions help you to articulate what you want to achieve, committing to your intentions and saying what you mean can require courage. As the following anecdote shows, you may discover previously unknown aspects about yourself from which you want to hide.

Karyn and George have been married for ten years. Karyn's parents were divorced and because money was tight when she was a child, Karyn has always felt financially insecure. As an adult, she looked subconsciously for men to provide for her, despite working and making a decent living herself.

George comes from a wealthy family and as a bachelor never needed to work for a living or had money worries. Karyn stopped working after she and George were married in order to run the home and raise their two children. She quickly became frustrated with George because the two of them have very different attitudes towards money and fiscal responsibility. His income is insufficient to support a family of four, and as George spends more and more money on his collections and hobbies, he puts Karyn and their children in a financially precarious position.

Karyn wants to fix the situation and knows that she has to talk to George, but she wants to get her intentions clear first. Thinking long and hard, she admits to herself that her main reasons for marrying George were financial security and to have a family. She loves him and wants the marriage to remain intact, but she still harbours a desire to be looked after. Living a financially sound and responsible life is very important to her.

She states her intentions out loud to reinforce them to herself. Her preparation increases her awareness of her values and gives her confidence in holding the difficult conversation. Despite her anxieties about George's reaction, Karyn tells him how she feels and that she's going to get a job to contribute to the family finances and put that money into a separate account to protect her earnings. She wants to be looked after in her marriage but knows that to achieve her goal of financial security, she has to make that happen herself. In addition to uncovering her insecurities, by articulating her intentions she also discovers her strengths.

When Karyn tells George her plans he feels threatened, because he wants to be able to provide for his family. As he and Karyn speak, he appreciates Karyn's clarity and commitment to the relationship. He also recognises that his strengths and interests lie in the domestic area of their lives rather than in working outside the home. He enjoys cooking more than Karyn does and is happy to run the household while Karyn re-establishes her career to provide additional income. By facing their situation together and recognising their individual strengths and the meaningful and satisfying contributions they each can make, George and Karyn are able to create an outcome which satisfies their needs.

Think about how you speak to your staff and employees. If you speak to them in an angry, irritable and impatient way, and your orders are conflicting, unclear and contradictory, you struggle to gain support from your staff. Not only are they unable to perform at their best for you, they don't want to.

Now, imagine that you're a boss who's clear and confident in what you expect from your staff. Your instructions are easy to follow. You're patient, kind and accepting. Not only are your staff members keen to help you, but also they want to; they're eager to help you achieve your goals.

Sometimes people say 'you know what I mean?' in an attempt to push listeners into deciphering what they mean when in fact they weren't being clear. At those times, you can help the speaker clarify by saying, 'I'm not sure that I understand your point. Would you mind rephrasing it for me?' This technique may irritate speakers by forcing them to turn their passive intentions into active ones, but that's okay because you're helping them to say what they mean.

In addition to having a clear intention when you speak, saying what you mean requires that you speak in ways that the listener understands. Filling your sentences with jargon, loading your phrases with unfamiliar terms and mumbling your way through a conversation doesn't help you convey your message in a clear, coherent and compelling way.

To help, think about your message from your listeners' points of view and how they may view the situation you're addressing. Choose and use words and phrases they understand. Speak clearly and concisely so they can follow what you mean. When the words you speak and the way you deliver them match, you help listeners understand what you mean. (In Chapter 7 I provide tips on articulating clearly and in Chapter 8 I look at ways of using your body language to support your spoken message.)

Meaning what you say

When you have a clear intention (as I describe in the preceding section) and speak with certainty and confidence, you come across as meaning what you say. As a result listeners believe you. To achieve this aim and engage with listeners you need to be firm in your choice of language and commit verbally, physically and emotionally to your thoughts, message and way of speaking. When you do so you're easier to understand than people who withhold their emotions and mumble.

When you saturate your sentences with *fillers* such as 'ers', 'ums' and 'ahs' and pepper your phrases with 'I think', 'I'll try', 'I guess', 'I hope' and 'like, you know' you sound unsure about your meaning and if you're not sure, your listeners certainly won't be either.

When you feel sounds such as 'um' and 'ah' and words such as 'I think' and 'I'll try' forming on your lips, purposely close your mouth and inhale through your nose. You may initially feel awkward, but your audience perceives you as being in control when you momentarily pause before making your next statement. Even better, you sound and feel like you're in control when you eliminate sounds that distract from your message.

Swapping phrases to make a point

Rhetoric is the art of conversation that speakers employ to motivate or persuade their listeners. One rhetorical technique you can use to draw attention to a particular point is to relate two or more clauses to each other by reversing the structure of the sentence. One of the best-known examples comes from *Alice's Adventures in Wonderland* by Lewis Carroll:

> Then you should say what you mean,' the March Hare went on.

'I do,' Alice hastily replied, 'at least. . .at least I mean what I say. . .that's the same thing, you know.'

'Not the same thing a bit!' said the Hatter. 'Why, you might just as well say that "I see what I eat" is the same thing as "I eat what I see"!'

A famous modern example is John F. Kennedy's 'Mankind must put an end to war or war will put an end to mankind.'

Edward had the habit of using vague and uncertain wording. Whether he said 'I'll try to call you' or 'hopefully, I'll have this report in by the end of the week' he sounded weak and his friends and colleagues doubted his intentions. Edward developed this habit as a protection against disappointing others. It gave him an 'out clause' so that if he didn't follow through he was able to offer an acceptable excuse. Sadly, his intention backfired on him and he gained a reputation for being inconsistent and not to be trusted.

When Edward realised this negative impact, he practised saying 'I will' instead of 'I'll try'. By making this alteration and a verbal commitment to his intention, he confirmed his commitment, and followed through on what he said he would do to prove that he's a man of his word. While following through is a habit Edward still struggles with, by changing his language pattern, he no longer gives himself an excuse for not doing what he says he's going to do.

As Yoda from the *Star Wars* films says, 'There is no try. There is only do.'

You can enhance your meaning by selecting specific descriptive words and examples for clarity. For example, instead of saying that you'd like your assistant to create a template for contracts, be explicit about the details, as in: 'I'd like separate sections that detail the company's terms and conditions, testimonials, client responsibilities, processes and expectations. In addition, I want you to highlight headings in the corporate colours and use the approved font.' Specifics leave little doubt about what you mean.

Make sure that these words aren't so erudite (ha!) that your listeners have to hot-foot it to their nearest dictionary to understand what you're talking about!

Presenting a Compelling Case

When you're trying to get a point across to achieve your desired outcome, you need to present a compelling case so that what you want makes sense to your listeners. You have to tap into their interests, passions or curiosity and be seen as credible, trustworthy and honest to compel your listener to pay attention to you. Otherwise, you're going to struggle to convince them that your message is worth considering.

The bottom line is that people are only interested in what you're saying if your points apply to them. A question often in people's heads as they're listening to your point is 'What is in it for me?' Selfish, perhaps, but certainly true; to present a compelling case you need to know what matters to your listeners.

In order to present a compelling case:

- ✔ Find common ground (check out Chapter 5).
- ✔ Connect at an emotional level (again, see Chapter 5).
- ✔ Send a message that resonates with your listener (as I discuss in Chapter 6).
- ✔ Listen with the intention to understand (flip to Chapter 4).

Tapping into what matters to the other person

To find out what matters to other people you have to ask questions, listen for understanding and tune in your observational antennae, which all require time, effort and patience as well as a sincere desire to learn. When you listen skilfully and demonstrate that you care about what's important to people, they're likely to share with you their thoughts, beliefs and feelings. By understanding others' values, beliefs and the concerns that they're facing, you have information that you can use to inform your approach.

When you're seeking to discover what matters to other people, ask yourself 'what's the benefit for my listeners?' If you're to be successful in presenting a compelling case, you have to address what matters to your listeners.

Speaking with credibility

To demonstrate credibility you need to be well-versed in the subject matter so that you can speak with authority. Also, ask yourself how listeners perceive you. How much do you know about their needs, concerns, values, beliefs and culture? Do you come across as honest and trustworthy, do you give an impression of integrity and ethical behaviour and are you believable?

In order for your listeners to believe what you say, you need to establish your credibility. Here are ideas for doing so:

✔ **Develop honest relationships:** Hidden agendas and withheld information compromise your credibility. Justify your point of view by addressing the pros and cons of an issue and explain your reasoning to validate your position.

✔ **Follow through on promises:** Whether you're promising your boss that you're going to meet her deadlines or promising your daughter that you're going to her dance recital, follow through. Failing to do so is a sure way of corroding your credibility. If unexpected circumstances get in the way, immediately set in place alternative plans to carry out your promise. Coming up with another arrangement demonstrates your desire to be true to your word.

✔ **Be consistent:** When you work for a business you represent that organisation's values and goals. Even when times are tough, stick to your guns, because if you change your position you tarnish your credibility. People who look up to you for guidance and direction start to doubt your ability and question themselves for having trusted you. People trust those who stand by their convictions.

✔ **Demonstrate respect by acknowledging the concerns of others:** People feel recognised when you show them that their feelings and the issues that they're facing are important to you and the organisation. Although you may not be able to solve their problems or meet their needs, treating them with respect and really listening to their concerns demonstrates that you're a credible person who can be trusted to do what you can to support them. (Turn to Chapter 4 for more on listening for understanding.)

✔ **Have proof in place:** When you make a point, state a concern or reveal a belief make sure that you have the facts close to hand. Backing up your position is vital for demonstrating your authority; making statements that you can't prove is a sure way to sabotage your credibility.

✔ **Uphold confidentiality:** When you show that you can be trusted to maintain confidentiality, you open the door to fearless conversation. People feel that they can talk to you about private matters without worrying about you spilling the beans or discounting what's important to them. Without trust, you compromise your credibility.

Removing Potential Barriers to Achieving Your Aims

Plenty of barriers can stand in the way of you communicating with clarity, composure and commitment and so prevent you from achieving your communication goals (see Figure 2-1):

✔ **External and environmental factors:** Time, temperature, noise, outmoded equipment and personal conflicts.

✔ **Internal factors:** Stress, lack of clarity, mood, attitude, distracting gestures, beliefs, biases, prejudices and relationships.

If you add even a few of these together you're bound to create the Berlin Wall of communication barriers.

The subject of 'barriers to communication' could fill a whole book and so I focus on three internal barriers – criticising, moralising and casting blame.

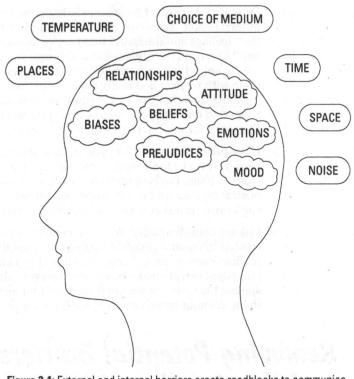

Figure 2-1: External and internal barriers create roadblocks to communication by confusing the listener and distracting the speaker.

Avoiding criticising

I've yet to find anyone who enjoys being criticised, but the fact is that you may have to provide constructive criticism from time to time to help people improve an area of their lives or work. Constructive criticism is valuable when given in a way the receiver can understand.

Focusing on behaviour rather than personal traits helps people improve their performance, modify their approach, enhance their productivity and progress their careers. In contrast, censuring, finding fault and judging people's personalities harshly is guaranteed to make them feel bad about themselves (and not think much of you either).

Keith's manager, David, communicates with his team in a way that leaves them feeling frustrated, insecure, demoralised and unfairly treated. Words such as 'stupid', 'lazy' and 'incompetent' are part of David's daily vocabulary. He fails to understand why his staff members seem dispirited when he just wants them to improve their results.

Keith (a highly regarded member of the team) begins to act out his dissatisfaction. Previously willing to go the extra mile for David, he becomes 'unavailable' when asked to do tasks outside his remit. He leaves the office early and turns reports in late. Eventually, Keith transfers to another department, headed by a manager who believes in praising results and criticising behaviour – not personality – when it negatively impacts on performance. After several members of his team complain about his managerial skills, David leaves the company.

Instead of criticising, look for ways to provide constructive feedback. Management guru and author Kenneth Blanchard, said, 'feedback is the breakfast of champions.' Feedback helps others to make informed decisions about how to behave and what issues to consider. In addition, providing insights into how people perform helps them understand the impact of their actions without casting blame for outcomes.

The purpose of providing feedback is to highlight the consequences of what you and others have observed. Aim to create connections between the actions of the person you're providing feedback to, other people's reactions and the likely consequences for the individual (though without in any way making the latter sound like threats). If the person you're providing feedback to resists your message or gets defensive, reconsider your approach; perhaps you're trying too hard to prove that you're right. If that happens, step back and rephrase your observations as opinions for consideration.

If you notice that people seem to have lost their enthusiasm for their jobs, focus on what they're doing correctly and praise them for their efforts. For the greatest effect, offer the praise immediately and make it specific. Assume that team members want to do a good job and provide encouragement rather than criticism.

Rolling eyes, disapproving facial expressions and negative noises are easily spotted by the person you're criticising. Instead, think how you'd like to be treated in that person's situation and remember that non-verbal behaviour speaks louder than words. Offering honest praise, as opposed to providing destructive criticism, is the most effective way to get the behaviour you're after.

Letting go of moralising

Even the most positive people eventually lose heart if you approach them with expressions such as, 'You should do this', 'You ought to. . .' and 'Why didn't you. . .'. Telling people what they should and shouldn't do sets up explicit rules that may ring true for you but not for others. Although rules, or a formal code of ethics, play a part at work – you can call these occupational responsibilities – in everyday life, no such code exists. Even the laws by which you and I live don't necessarily conform to individuals' moral beliefs.

Diplomats understand that although they can describe people's perceptions of moral issues, the last thing they want to do is judge these perceptions in terms of right or wrong. If they did they'd lose their jobs and possibly start a war. If you start moralising and judging others you can expect them to return the favour. And how would that make you feel?

When you're tempted to tell people what they should or shouldn't do, follow my grandmother's advice (though she may have got it from someone more famous!): 'Judge not lest ye be judged.' Believe me you're more likely to achieve what you want when you do.

Casting aside blame

Playing the blame game allows you to avoid taking respon-sibility and action. Blaming others when things go wrong makes you sound hostile, abrasive and confrontational. This is no way to communicate successfully, unless your goal is to create upset and discord. When you speak in positive terms that enable others to take responsibility for their behaviour, you come across as constructive, credible and respectful because your aim is to reduce conflict, enhance communica-tion and decrease defensiveness.

The way you express yourself affects how people receive your message. When you use positive language you're more likely to elicit co-operation than confrontation because you project a helpful, positive image rather than a destructive, negative one.

Identifying and eliminating negative language helps you to move towards positive communication, free of blame. Then you're able to replace the accusing language with helpful ways of conveying the same information. Take a look at Table 2-1: the examples in the left-hand column imply carelessness, blame and even dishonesty. By replacing them with phrases such as those in the right-hand column, you create a co-operative, blameless approach.

Table 2-1	Replacing Accusing Language with Positive Phrases
Blame-inducing Phrases	*Blameless Phrases*
'You failed to include. . .'	'May I suggest that. . .'
'You overlooked enclosing. . .'	'I can't seem to find. . .'
'You claim that. . .'	'One option open to you is. . .'
'You say that. . .'	'We can help you. . .'
'You state that. . .'	'What you could consider is. . .'

Review some of your previous memos or emails. Go through each one carefully, highlighting words, phrases and sentences that have a negative, blaming tone. Pay special attention to subtle aspects of your message that may send bureaucratic or demeaning messages. Then, rewrite the memo or email using positive, constructive language.

When you blame others you give up your personal power. Instead, when things go wrong help them to recognise their responsibility so that they, and you, can learn from the identified behaviours.

Chapter 3

Valuing Different Communication Styles

In This Chapter

▶ Deciphering communication differences

▶ Adapting your own style as necessary

Although you may find people who're different from you frustrating, annoying or simply confusing, being able to accept, appreciate and work with diverse communication styles enhances your relationships and produces positive results in your personal and professional life. Instead of focusing on the difficulties of communicating with people whose style is different from yours, consider the strength that can come with diversity. If you're able to keep an open mind to the various styles you encounter in your daily life, you can see opposite points of view and connect with others in a positive and productive way.

In this chapter I discuss some different communication preferences you may encounter and show you how to adapt your style to communicate with comfort and confidence.

Developing Your Awareness of Different Communication Styles

No doubt you've noticed that some people seem easy to communicate with while others present you with challenges. The reason is because everyone has a preferred way of communicating. If you can recognise and respect the way people prefer to communicate without judging their approach, you're well on your way to communicating with ease and effectiveness.

Endless variations and mixtures of personality types and communication preferences exist (as I explain in the nearby sidebar 'Knowing me, knowing you'), far too many to cover in one short chapter. Therefore, I focus on just two common groups of communication styles:

- ✓ **Extrovert/introvert:** Some people are forthright and direct in their speaking and talk while they think, whereas others remain quiet until they're sure of what they're saying (to find out more, flip to 'Communicating with the loud and proud or the meek and mild' later in this chapter).

- ✓ **Fine detail/big picture:** Some individuals focus closely on the minutiae and detailed facts of a subject, whereas others look at the larger picture, often relying on metaphors and analogies to make their points (check out the later section 'Taking in the wide view or preferring detail').

Each style has its strengths and weaknesses. When you acknowledge and accept that the expression 'one man's ceiling is another man's floor' can apply to communication styles, you're able to communicate in a way that satisfies your own and other people's requirements.

Work on becoming aware of and appreciating people whose styles are different from yours. Then, instead of spending time fault-finding and struggling to communicate, you can sit back, relax and know that strength resides in differences.

Communicating with the loud and proud or the meek and mild

One group of people who seem at opposite ends of the communication spectrum are fast-talking extroverts and more thoughtful introverts. Recognising these different approaches and tendencies helps you communicate with such people whatever their style and your own.

Knowing me, knowing you

Personality is a hugely complex topic that has been considered for thousands of years, from ancient civilisations (such as the Egyptians and Mesopotamians with their concept of physical and mental health being connected to the elements of fire, water, earth and air) via Carl Jung in the 19th century and Katherine Briggs and Isabel Myers' 20th-century work on personality differences (the Myers Briggs Type Inventory), to the modern-day psychology of David Keirsey's personality assessment. The more you draw from research and theories, the better able you are to understand yourself, which better positions you to motivate, inspire and work effectively with teams and individuals. To find out more about personality differences and psychology, pick up a copy of *Psychology For Dummies* by Adam Cash (Wiley).

Most studies agree that innate nature combined with nurture produces personality. Although people have different personality and communication preferences, all mentally healthy people are able to adapt their styles according to the situation, even if some are more willing and flexible in doing so than others. When you combine awareness with adaptability – understanding personality types and the related behaviour in yourself and others – you're in the driver's seat. The ability to adapt according to various situations is undoubtedly the most powerful and useful capability you can possess.

Giving the introvert time to think

Introverts take their time to speak. They need to consider their views and process their opinions before sharing them with the world. With their strong powers of concentration and ability to analyse data, including facts, figures and situations, introverts are most comfortable when they're given time to reflect before articulating their ideas.

In general, introverts are invigorated by quiet conversations that allow time for contemplation. They draw energy from their own internal resources, including their ideas, emotions and impressions. In the best of all possible worlds, they're most comfortable keeping their thoughts and ideas to themselves. They prefer solitude and become drained by too much social interaction.

Extroverts, however, are stimulated by lively enthusiastic discussions and rapid-paced conversations. As a result they find the conversational pace of introverts slow and laborious while they take time to build their thoughts and ideas internally. (Check out the later 'Letting the extrovert take the stage' section to discover more about how extroverts communicate.) Because introverts and extroverts are energised and drained in the opposite way, expect communication challenges when the two get together.

Introverts share information only after they carefully think it through and evaluate it. They function best when they have time to think and reflect.

Instead of judging introverts for being reclusive and slow off the mark, value them for the thought and consideration they bring to their observations. You can count on introverts to come up with well-thought-out responses, as long as you give them time to think.

Amy is an analyst for an investment bank. At work she's known for her powers of concentration and ability to reflect and behave in a careful and cautious way before voicing her opinions. She tends to seek out quiet areas in order to concentrate on her work and gets annoyed by phone calls and other interruptions when she's deep in thought.

At meetings she tends to speak in a hesitant manner and requires time to think before responding to questions. Her need to reflect before presenting her conclusions means that her boss and some of her colleagues get frustrated with her and frequently complain that she never contributes at meetings and is slow to make decisions. But Amy simply wants to make sure that she has time to consider the facts before presenting her conclusions.

Introverts prefer to internalise information before responding and so you can trust that when they do speak they've carefully evaluated the details and considered their responses. When possible, aim to arrange a one-to-one meeting in which they're more comfortable communicating their opinions than in large groups. Be sure to invite them to speak in meetings and at events, because they much prefer written over oral communication. For example, you can advise them in advance of a meeting and what contribution you'd like them to make. You can also let them know that it's okay for them to say something along the lines of, 'I'd like to consider what I've heard and will come back to you via email with my thoughts.' By acknowledging their communication style, you avoid putting them on the spot and making them feel uncomfortable. Before a performance review, give them plenty of notice because being prepared means that introverts are less likely to shut down in the face of criticism (compared to coming into a situation cold). Perhaps even send them some questions in advance.

People can think of introverts as being shy, withdrawn, nerdy, unfriendly and antisocial. But in fact they like people and just need time on their own to charge their batteries.

For a fascinating talk about introversion, tune into `www.ted.com/talks/lang/en/susan_cain_the_power_of_introverts.html`.

Leaders who prefer solitude

Research reveals that the ratio of introverts to extroverts in the world is one to three, and four in ten top executives (including Microsoft's Bill Gates, movie mogul Steven Spielberg and business magnate Warren Buffett) are presumed to be introverted. Introverts in leadership roles often put their success down to the fact that they have an inner core of strength and think before they act. Although introverts may struggle to progress their careers if their quiet demeanour is seen as uninspiring, in the right organisations their preference for solitude is perceived as calm, composed and circumspect.

One of the most obvious ingredients for success is an outgoing, gregarious personality, and so successful introverts often discover how to take on extrovert characteristics. For example, Brenda Barnes, former CEO of Sarah Lee Corporation and the first female CEO of Pepsi-Cola, describes this ability as being like an 'out of body experience' that allows introverts to observe themselves being uninhibited and outgoing for a brief while.

In his 2001 bestseller, *Good to Great*, Jim Collins reports that most companies have CEOs who are self-effacing and humble to a fault rather than seekers of the limelight. Research also shows that introverts are among the most creative people and that creativity is the one trait most frequently shared by highly successful leaders.

Letting the extrovert take the stage

People who demonstrate a preference for interacting with others and seeking stimulation from outside of themselves are referred to as extroverts. They tend to have a breadth of interests, talk freely about what's on their minds and like to be actively involved with people and events.

Extroverts are comfortable presenting themselves in a public forum, whether at a business meeting or dinner party. They aren't afraid to speak up, and frequently do with no inhibitions. Although they're comfortable with lots going on around them, they can be easily distracted.

If you're working with extroverts, allow them to become involved with other people and participate in activities. Leaving them on their own for too long, bereft of interactions with other people, causes them to feel agitated and restless for company. They can get energised by interruptions, such as phone calls and office chitchat, and become impatient and bored when their work is repetitive. They work best when presented with tasks that require engaging with others and taking action rather than long periods of solitary concentration and reflection.

Extroverts like to talk through ideas and struggle to keep their thoughts to themselves. Their style tends to be energetic, enthusiastic and excitable, and they have a reputation of throwing caution to the wind. When asked questions they respond quickly and tend to think out-loud, sharing their thoughts and experiences almost as quickly as they happen.

Some people label extroverts (often wrongly) as superficial because of their tendency to fill the space with the sound of their own voices. They tend to jump into discussions – some may say they interrupt – and finish other people's sentences for them. Yet they embrace new relationships with ease, have oodles of energy and like to be on the go.

Kristina and Kelly work in marketing for a hedge fund. One day they're assigned to work together on a marketing project, writing for potential customers about a new investment fund their company is launching. Both of the women are extroverts and tackle the task by talking about the product at length. Their method is to approach customers to gain information, including what they want to know about new products. They also interview other marketing professionals to gather more information about how best to market complicated financial instruments.

When they have their data in place they speak with the fund managers to make sure that they understand the details and have their facts correct. Before writing a word, they talk extensively through their concept. Only when they're confident that their ideas are arranged do they begin to write, recording their concept on a dictating machine. As extroverts, their approach is to talk first, write later.

Taking in the wide view or preferring detail

Some people naturally see problems and situations in a general manner, as if through a wide-angle lens; others seem to have close-up sight, focusing automatically in a narrower way. Both tendencies have their different strengths, as I describe in this section.

Picking up on the big picture

People with a 'sixth sense' tend to rely on hunches, intuition and gut feelings. They notice possibilities within a situation and make associations between one piece of information and another. What excites and stimulates them are future possibilities and change, not life's little details.

Big-picture thinkers tend to:

- ✔ Be restless, appreciating and enjoying new and different experiences.

- ✔ Get annoyed when things are defined in too much detail, preferring generalisations and approximations.

- ✔ Skip over the fine print and count on insight, inspiration and imagination to create answers.

- ✔ Be creative, strategic and visionary, but can also be messy, disorganised and forgetful.

According to legend, Albert Einstein never wore socks. Even when he dined at the US White House his feet were bare, except for his shoes. He believed that shaving and brushing his hair was a waste of time and his desk was notoriously messy. As far as Einstein was concerned, life's little practicalities were irritating and not worth bothering with. As he stated, 'The only valuable thing is intuition.' Instead of spending his time clearing his cupboards and sharpening his pencils, Einstein worked on perfecting the theory of relativity.

Here are some typical characteristics of big-picture types:

- They're able to see patterns quickly in complex problems.
- They can assimilate information from a large number of seemingly unrelated sources.
- They have a passion for coming up with new ideas and projects.
- They exhibit low tolerance for detailed work, such as filling out forms and tedious tasks.
- They take in the broad brush outline of a situation but struggle with the fine details.

Don't expect a conversation with big-picture thinkers to be focused on facts and details, because general concepts excite them more than concrete examples. Therefore, prepare yourself for theoretical exchanges laced with metaphors and analogies, in which insights and possibilities drive the discussion and digressions are inevitable (given half a chance, they prefer to take a roundabout approach to presenting information). These individuals rely on instinct and imagination to fuel their arguments and seek innovative, atypical and challenging suggestions. As a result, big-picture thinkers opt for change and seek a life beyond the obvious.

Appreciating other people's style and adapting yours to meet theirs in order to achieve mutually satisfying goals is a hallmark of great communicators. While being flexible may be a challenge, making the effort is worth the price, as Kate and Jonathan's story demonstrates.

Like many happily married couples, Kate and Jonathan approach life quite differently. Kate is a big-picture thinker who embraces change and challenges, while Jonathan seeks predictability, the status quo and fine detail. What Kate sees as possibilities, Jonathan views as drawbacks. While looking to buy a family home they come upon Kate's dream house: a rambling Edwardian property. Kate has visions of their future children running up and down the central staircase and the laughter of friends and family filling the halls. Although the house and gardens have long been neglected, Kate isn't deterred.

Knowing that Jonathan is put off by the state of the property Kate focuses her husband's attention on the aspects of the house that will appeal to him. Avoiding the state of the electrics and the plumbing, she points out the period features, including the hardwood floors and stained-glass windows, which are all in good shape. She shows him the detached workroom where he can build his model boats. Knowing Jonathan will be concerned about the practical costs of restoration, Kate puts together a plan. She speaks with several builders and gathers estimates. She explains to Jonathan how the costs of the property per square metre compare to the small, newly built homes on a modern estate that Jonathan favours. In addition, Kate points out the resale value of living in a historic part of town and helps him visualise future family traditions, such as summer parties in the garden and Sunday lunches in the grand dining room.

Although careful reasoning is not Kate's preferred style, she knows that by taking this approach she can convince Jonathan to purchase the old property. Through inspired remodelling it meets his need for tradition and practicality while satisfying her desire to apply her creativity and imagination. Jonathan is satisfied with the current state of the property, but Kate continues to have ideas for more improvements. (For more about people who prefer realism over imagination, like Jonathan, check out the following section.)

Focusing on the fine detail

When people prefer to pay attention to information they gather through their five senses, you can trust that they believe and rely on the facts and details of a situation (unlike big-picture thinkers who prefer their instincts, as I describe in the preceding section). Fine-detail people put their faith in practical information with useful applications and base their decisions on firm data and not intuition. They like to live their lives in the here-and-now, in an orderly fashion, and prefer tried-and-tested solutions to problems.

You can spot fine-detail people by the attention they pay to specifics, firm evidence and undisputable facts. During conversations, they concentrate on particular elements and practical matters. They seek realistic applications of data and illustrate and illuminate their points through personal experience. If the conversation takes a turn towards insights and possibilities, they become uncomfortable.

When speaking with people who focus on detail, avoid generalities and stick to hard data. Make sure that your suggestions are straightforward, realistic and practical.

These fine-detail observers:

✔ Have the ability to focus on the particulars of a situation.

✔ Can't see the forest for the trees.

✔ Prefer to edit a plan than to devise the original.

✔ Tend to over-think.

✔ Pay attention to what's happening in the present.

Make sure that you allow people who focus on detail to apply skills that they've already developed instead of insisting that they learn new ones. Remember that they prefer to have all the facts in place before starting a project, they tend to distrust inspiration and bright ideas that can't be backed up with facts. Take advantage of their preference for work that has a practical aspect to it.

Paula and Irene own an events management company and have been asked to organise the annual awards ceremony for one of their long-standing clients. Although the client has been satisfied with their work in the past, he's looking for something different this year.

Paula is a detail-oriented person who likes to start with facts and then form the big picture. Her preference is to consider the essence of a challenge – including its financial implications – and stick to the tried and true. As a result she's uncomfortable with the lack of direction in the brief, other than to produce something 'innovative and exciting'. In contrast, Irene is thrilled. Unlike Paula, who likes to work from experience, Irene revels in the opportunity to create something original.

The good news is that because they've worked together for many years, the women trust one another to play their parts. While Irene leaps from one possibility to the next and comes up with ground-breaking ideas, Paula applies her pragmatic way of thinking and keeps the project grounded.

Adapting Your Style for Clear Communication

If everyone saw the world in the same way, life would be pretty bland. The beauty of differences is that people can enrich their lives by considering perspectives they may not normally contemplate. Opposites attract because their differences create a mutually beneficial symbiotic relationship, with each enhancing the other's gifts.

Although opposite styles can create a powerful force when working together, communication between people who view the world or get energised differently can sometimes be difficult. (Read the earlier section 'Developing Your Awareness of Different Communication Styles' for loads more on such differences.) To help, in this section I provide some tips for getting other people to understand you and for you to better understand them.

Helping others to understand what you mean

> *I know that you believe you understand what you think I said, but I'm not sure you realise that what you heard is not what I meant.*

> — Robert McCloskey, United States career diplomat

When you pay attention to how others communicate you can figure out what their preferences are and adapt your style accordingly. (For more about how to listen effectively, turn to Chapter 4). Here's an easy three-step approach to being understood:

1. **Become aware of how you communicate.** For example, ask yourself whether you talk quickly and dramatically with few pauses or prefer to speak only after due consideration. Also consider whether you like to focus on the specifics of a situation or prefer to discuss options and possibilities.

2. **Know how the people listening to you prefer to communicate.** For example, do they seem thoughtful and attentive or are they straining to interrupt? Do they offer you detailed analysis or explore visions and potential?

3. **Put these two pieces of information together to create a communication style.** Ensure that you share your message so that listeners can understand what you're saying in the way you mean them to.

So, if you're a fast talker who leaps from topic to topic and you notice that your listeners look like rabbits caught in the headlights, slow down and make your points in fine detail; don't count on people to follow your rapid chain of thought.

Similarly, remember that introverts need time to think before answering. Their stillness doesn't necessarily mean that they're bored (though that can happen if you fail to engage with them). Recognise that they're formulating their response and give them plenty of space to reflect after you speak.

Seeing things from someone else's point of view

To communicate effectively with others, you may have to work on seeing things the way they do. Doing so can feel awkward, unnatural and uncomfortable, but the more you practise, the easier the behaviour becomes.

Extroverts focus on people, things and action and are energised by what happens in the external world. So if this doesn't come naturally to you, work on conversations that reflect other people's interests and passions. If you're an introvert, be prepared to share personal information about yourself to build relationships and rehearse speaking as quickly as you can.

Along the same lines, if you're a big-picture visionary who's reliant on inspiration, practise narrowing your focus on detail, the present reality and your past experiences (for more, um, detail, flip to the earlier section 'Focusing on the fine detail').

Part II
Being Receptive to Others

'I paraphrased for clarity and then
they let me know I'd been heard
and understood.'

In this part...

To communicate effectively, you have to develop some necessary skills. Here I show you how to listen with the intention of understanding, so you can really get to grips with what's important to other people and respond to their needs. I also give you insider tips for building trusting and honest relationships.

Chapter 4

Listening Actively for Total Understanding

In This Chapter

▶ Figuring out what someone means

▶ Listening with empathy

▶ Treating others with respect

I'd like to ask you some questions. Have you ever wanted to state an observation without someone judging or evaluating what you're saying? Do you long to express your needs, values and feelings straight from your heart without fear of reprisal? And what about making a request knowing that your listeners are interpreting your message the way that you want them to? If your answer to any of these questions is yes, then you're not alone. I guess that everyone reading this chapter longs to be listened to without being assessed, criticised or misunderstood.

More often than not, when people are listening they're distracted, thinking about something else or considering their responses to what they've just heard. When you practise active listening, however, you focus solely on the speaker, pay attention and respond while letting go of your own point of view. You shelve your personal judgements and avoid internal distractions in order to give the person speaking your unbiased and undivided attention.

People who listen actively, foster personal relationships filled with understanding and co-operation, free of controversy and discord. They comprehend, retain and respond to what the other person is expressing. Active listeners pay attention not only to what's being said, but also listen for how the message is being expressed, as well as for those messages behind the words that aren't being articulated verbally. People who listen actively are outstanding communicators.

In this chapter you discover techniques for listening in the way that you want others to listen to you. You uncover ways of understanding, interpreting and evaluating what you hear without your own feelings, needs and desires blocking your reception. You find out how to get people to open up, avoid misunderstandings, resolve conflict and build trust. In addition, by practising active listening, you improve your productivity at work and enhance your ability to influence, persuade and negotiate with success.

Listening with the Intention to Understand

In his book *The 7 Habits of Highly Successful People*, Stephen Covey says, 'Seek first to understand, then to be understood.' At the core of active listening is the desire to understand what someone else wants to communicate.

When you're listening, keep in mind that often people don't say everything they're thinking and feeling. To get the full meaning of what's being communicated, you have to pay particular attention to non-verbal behaviour including the tone, pace and pitch of the other person's voice as well as body language and the words used. You can find out more about how non-verbal behaviour conveys messages in my book *Body Language For Dummies* (Wiley).

In order to understand, pay careful attention to the words being spoken and the way that the speaker is delivering them.

Giving speakers your undivided attention shows that you respect them enough to listen to what they have to say. When you treat people with respect they're more likely to listen to you when your time comes to speak.

When you give someone your undivided attention you can understand that person's perspective. As a result, when you know what people are thinking and feeling, communicating with them is easier than if you've no idea what they're talking about.

Here are some simple tips for improving your listening skills:

- **Face the speaker:** Lean slightly forward to demonstrate that you're paying attention to what the other person is saying.

- **Maintain eye contact:** Look at other people while they're speaking to you to let them know that you're engaged in the conversation.

  Refrain from staring because that can make you both uncomfortable. You don't want to come across as creepy!

- **Minimise external distractions:** Turn off the television, shut down your computer, stop reading and put your electronic gadgets away.

- **Turn off your internal chatter:** Let go of your judgements, defences and prejudices and focus on what the speaker is saying – the words and the behaviour.

- **Respond with interest:** Nod and from time to time inject expressions such as, 'I see,' 'Tell me more' or 'Really, that's interesting.' Ask questions along the lines of, 'How did that make you feel?', 'Then what happened?', 'What would you have liked to have happened?' Even a simple murmured 'uh-huh' and 'um-mmm' can make the listener feel that you're engaged.

- **Keep an open mind:** Refrain from making assumptions about what the speaker is thinking and avoid interrupting with your own point of view until the other person finishes talking.

- **Let people make their point:** Even if someone is criticising you, allow the person to finish before reacting or defending yourself. In this way people feel as if they've made their point and don't need to repeat it, and you clearly understand that point of view before responding.

- **Become engaged in conversations:** Ask questions to clarify your understanding but only after people are finished; that way you don't interrupt their train of thought. After they finish speaking, paraphrase what they say by starting off with, 'So, you're saying. . .' or 'What I understood you to say is. . .'. Check out the later section 'Paraphrasing for clarity' for more on this topic.

Lowering your barriers

Sometimes you don't want to hear what someone has to say, especially when the message hurts or threatens you. At these times you may physically turn away, tell other people that you don't care what they think or, in worst-case scenarios, say that you don't think what they're saying is worth listening to.

If you put up such barriers when you're listening, you limit your chances of facing complicated issues in your relationships and reduce your ability to solve complex problems. Lowering your barriers allows you to understand what other people are talking about as well as how they think and feel.

When someone is offering you a few home truths, no matter how painful they are to accept, listen with the intention of understanding the other person's point of view. Open yourself up to the possibility that hearing it may be good for you.

Barriers to listening actively include, but aren't limited to, the following:

✔ **Assumptions:** Because the human mind can process a lot of information more quickly than people speak, you may interrupt the person speaking because you think you know what that person is about to say. When you make such an assumption, you're creating a conclusion based on partial information. No matter how tempting, refrain from speaking until the other person has finished. Then pause to show that you've absorbed what's been said before offering your opinion.

✔ **Defensiveness:** If you seek to protect yourself from criticism you place barriers between yourself and the messages other people are sending. Instead of viewing comments and criticisms as personal attacks, use the messages as an instrument for self-assessment, improvement and personal development.

✔ **Ego:** If you think that you've nothing to learn from what someone else is saying, or that you're better than the other person, you close yourself off and stop listening. Although you may not agree with what's being said, keeping your mind open may allow you to discover something you didn't know before.

- ✔ **Environmental distractions:** These distractions can be your own internal messages, including pre-judging the other person's point of view, or issues that are concerning you that have nothing to do with the person speaking. They can also include electronic gadgets and the room temperature. Put away your toys, let go of unproductive thoughts and make yourself comfortable in order to listen properly to what the other person is saying.

- ✔ **Intolerance:** If you close your mind to the beliefs and opinions of others, you stand little chance of hearing what they're saying and the messages beneath the spoken word. If you really want to understand other people and build a strong relationship with them, put yourself in their shoes and see how the world seems from their perspective.

Letting go of judgement

If you really want to reflect that you understand what someone is saying and help the other person feel accepted and understood, let go of whatever judgements you may be holding. Whether you're judging the other person, the subject matter or their opinions, such assessments get in the way of listening to understand.

Your goal when actively listening is to pay complete attention to the person speaking, including word choice, tone of voice and body language, as well as appreciating their point of view. When you relinquish your judgements about people or the topic that they're talking about, you demonstrate a willingness to listen to their inner experience. The more you empathise as you listen, the more you're able to engage with what people are feeling and expressing – and the more they feel understood, the more willing they are to listen to you.

People have rights to their own feelings, thoughts and points of view! Try to refrain from analysing, interrupting, judging or giving advice too often, to avoid trampling over them.

When you let go of judging others while they're speaking, they feel that they've been heard, are less anxious about putting across their point of view and more likely to listen to or comply with what you have to say.

Turning off your opinions

The truth is that your own opinions on a topic can get in the way of learning. You can get caught up in thinking that your opinion is more valuable than what other people are saying and, in your impatience, cut them off before they complete their thoughts. If your experiences are anything like mine, you know how irritating it is when people offer their opinions before allowing you to offer yours.

Try not to interrupt by saying that you disagree with what people are saying before letting them finish. Give yourself the chance of learning their point of view to avoid the conversation grinding to a standstill or ending in an outright argument.

Improve your listening skills by waiting three seconds after the speaker finishes before replying. When your time comes to speak, ask supportive questions or seek clarification of the speaker's points. Don't make any points of your own during this exercise. Make sure that your questions are designed to gain understanding and not to express your own views.

The best communicators keep their minds open and receptive. They embrace opportunities to learn new insights and ideas and aren't afraid to listen to what other people have to say.

Paying attention to people's words and behaviours

I'm sure that from time to time you've heard someone say 'I'm great!' and yet noticed that they don't look great: their facial muscles are slack, their eyes are dull and their tone of voice is flat. When you spot an inconsistency between what's being said and the way the message is being expressed, take heed. The way people speak, including the words they use, the expression on their faces and the way their bodies move, conveys their state of mind.

To become an expert listener, concentrate on the non-verbal messages, including the voice – pitch, pace and tone – and body language – gestures, expressions and posture. Studies show that non-verbal behaviour can account for up to 93 per cent of the message the person is really conveying, whether intentionally or not. When in doubt, focus on the voice and the body to understand more fully what's going on for the other person's attitude, beliefs and point of view.

As well as paying attention to people's non-verbal behaviour, notice the words they choose to use too. Do they seem positive (glass half-full types) or negative (glass half-empty sorts)? The type of language people use conveys their attitudes, beliefs and mental states:

✔ **Negative language** tells the listener what can't be done, carries a subtle tone of blame, disparagement and scepticism and focuses on negative consequences.

✔ **Positive language** looks at possibilities, choices, options and alternatives. It sounds helpful and encouraging and stresses positive actions as well as focusing on anticipated positive outcomes.

Table 4-1 contains some examples of negative and positive language.

Table 4-1 Comparing Negative and Positive Phrases

Negative	Positive
It'll never work	Let's look at our options
The person's an idiot	This person sees things differently
You made me do it	I chose to do it

Hearing what people don't say

In order to hear what someone *isn't* saying, you have to want to understand what's important to the person. Then, you need to fine-tune your intuition to grasp the attitudes, feelings and beliefs that the speaker is harbouring. Appreciating another person's feelings requires you to connect with your own emotions in order to recognise other people's. For example, if you notice someone seems self-conscious, uncomfortable or embarrassed and you can recall feeling a similar emotion, you're more able to empathise than if you ignored, denied or were simply unaware of your feelings. (See my book *Persuasion & Influence For Dummies* (Wiley) for tips and techniques for establishing an emotional connection.)

Sometimes people don't want to tell you everything that they're feeling. They may feel hurt, embarrassed or insecure and don't want to share those feelings, or they may be concerned about the consequences of being open. By focusing on *how* people are communicating you're able to absorb information that they aren't articulating. I'm not suggesting that you intrude into their emotional and private life, but rather that you demonstrate care and consideration. As long as you're giving speakers your full, unbiased attention, you can pick up on the unspoken messages and respond to them with empathy and respect. Turn to Chapter 6 for ways of engaging with empathy.

When you're listening to people speak, pay particular attention to their movements and expressions to gain insights into the feeling behind the words. Tune into their voice, focusing on the rate, rhythm, volume and tone. The sharper your senses, the more you're able to hear what's not being said.

Getting into the Other Person's Mindset

Great communicators want to know what matters to other people. They pay attention to speakers' words and non-verbal behaviours in order to understand what they're saying and feeling. As I describe in this section, they confirm their understanding by asking questions, paraphrasing and summarising what's been said.

Asking questions to check your understanding

One of the earliest and greatest lessons I learned as a coach and consultant was to ask insightful questions. Only by confirming my understanding of a client's needs and concerns can I be of service to the individual and, if appropriate, the organisation.

Asking *open-ended questions* – those that can't be answered with a straightforward 'yes' or a 'no' – is the simplest way of checking your understanding and gaining further information. Questions that ask 'when, where, how, who' help you to understand the other person, because they encourage people to add more details, including their feelings, beliefs and attitudes.

In addition to open-ended questions, use the following phrases to gain more information and demonstrate that you're interested in the other person's thoughts, issues and problems:

✔ 'Tell me about. . .'

✔ 'I'm interested in hearing more about. . .'

✔ 'What I understand you're saying is. . .'

Paraphrasing for clarity

Paraphrasing what someone tells you is a must-have skill as regards establishing trust and promoting a constructive dialogue. Paraphrasing, which some people refer to as rephrasing, ensures that no misunderstandings exist and that you and the speaker are 'on the same page'. When you paraphrase other people's stories in your own words you have the chance to gain further information by encouraging them to clarify and expand on what they're saying. Restating the information you receive also demonstrates that you're interested in their point of view and what they're feeling.

Here are some examples of paraphrasing:

✔ 'So what you're saying is that you think the situation could've been handled better?'

✔ 'Are you saying that you weren't pleased with the approach they took?'

✔ 'So you're a bit let down by the result?'

✔ 'So you think that you'd feel more secure if they came with you?'

✔ 'What I hear you say is. . .'

As in most things in life, timing is of the essence. Avoid potential paraphrasing pitfalls by picking the right moment to feed back what you've heard and be tactful in your delivery to avoid antagonising someone whose emotions may be running high.

Frequently, when people are experiencing negative emotions, they use aggressive or defensive language that can damage relationships and cut off communication. Reporters are also known for trying to get interviewees to repeat language that can create a big soundbite. By paraphrasing – rather than directly repeating – 'loaded' language or connotations you demonstrate your understanding and validate the emotions behind the statement while phrasing the words in a more positive, less emotional way.

During an interview between ABC reporter Robert Krulwich and Russ Mittermeier, the then president of Conservation International, one of the world's largest environmental non-profit organisations with a diverse Board of Directors, Krulwich tried to get Mittermeier to describe the Board as 'radical' as a way of gaining a powerful soundbite. Mittermeier, a seasoned spokesperson, refused to grab the bait, no matter how hard Krulwich tried. When Krulwich said, 'Your Board is somewhat radical, yes?' Mittermeier responded with, 'I wouldn't say that. I'd say they're passionate, engaged and forward-thinking.' Krulwich tried again by saying, 'But if you define radical as passionate, engaged and forward-thinking, they're pretty radical, right?' Again, Mittermeier refused to accept Krulwich's clever paraphrasing in his attempt to put words into the spokesperson's mouth by responding, 'I wouldn't use that word.' Not once did Mittermeier utter the word 'radical', because to have done so would have damaged the reputation of the organisation, and the word wasn't a correct description of the Board. Because Krulwich's paraphrase wasn't accurate, Mittermeier refused to accept the loaded language.

When you paraphrase what someone's said, be sure to check your understanding. Never assume that your rephrasing is correct until speakers confirm that you've grasped their meaning. Asking if you correctly understand what the other person means, such as saying, 'Is that right?' or 'Am I correct in understanding that. . .?' or 'So, what I'm hearing you say is. . .' lets the other person know you're doing your best to grasp the meaning of what's being communicated.

Negotiating a night on the town

Nick's daughter, Penny, had been invited to a party and wanted to stay out later than Nick was comfortable with. When he told her that he'd like her to be home from the party by 1 a.m., Penny went ballistic.

She told her father that the party didn't end until 2 a.m. and that she had to stay to the end. Nick rephrased what he was hearing by saying that the party sounded like a big deal to Penny and that being there until the end was important to her. Penny replied, 'Totally! Ted will be there, there's going to be a live DJ and all my friends will be there! Dad, you just have to let me stay until the party's over!' Nick responded by saying, 'I hear that you're excited about the party and want to be there with Ted and your friends.' Penny repeated that she really was excited and wanted to be there for the whole party. Nick replied, 'I get that this party matters a lot to you and I'm concerned about your safety. I need to hear more details about the party – how you plan to get there and back – and figure out a solution that we're both comfortable with.'

By rephrasing what he heard Penny say, Nick showed that he understood what was important to his daughter.

Letting People Know They've Been Heard

The secret to being a great communicator is being a great listener. When people know that they've been heard – that their thoughts, feelings and ideas are understood – they're more open to engaging with you. Letting people know that you've really heard them is a gift you can give by focusing on what they say and rephrasing what you hear to confirm your understanding.

When you listen for feelings as well as facts, when you're willing to be corrected if you misunderstand the message and, most of all, when you treat others with respect, people are drawn to you like a wannabe celeb to a camera!

Being open to being corrected

Even if you're listening with the best intentions of understanding the other person's point of view and being non-judgemental (skills I describe in the earlier section 'Listening with the Intention to Understand'), and by wanting to validate the person's feelings (check out the preceding section), you may still occasionally get the wrong end of the stick. At those times, listen to the feedback the speaker gives you and don't argue the point. Thank them for their feedback and ask more questions for clarification. Asking for an example of what you did always helps to clarify. By being open to correction you demonstrate your respect for the speaker and your willingness to do whatever you can to enhance the communication.

If you interpret someone correcting your understanding of what they've said as a personal attack, you can become defensive and reply with a negative comment that curtails the conversation or escalates it down a negative path. Always remember that the point of the communication is to gain understanding. The earlier section 'Lowering your barriers' contains loads more on not sounding defensive and how to remove obstacles to active listening.

Going beneath what's been said

If you think that you can find out more than a speaker is telling you, ask probing questions that provide clarification and ensure that you've heard and understood the person's whole story. These questions can be as simple as asking for an example to help you understand something the speaker said. I say more about asking questions skilfully in the earlier section 'Asking questions to check your understanding'.

Probing questions can also elicit information when you believe that people are avoiding telling you something. If you sense that someone is purposely holding back information, such as covering feelings or withholding important facts, ask questions to delve more deeply and discover what lies beneath what's been said. Always demonstrate tact and empathy when questioning someone who seems to be resisting or avoiding answering your questions. Sometimes people don't want to answer your questions because they feel uncomfortable sharing private information with you. By backing off, you show that you understand. That being said, there are times when you have to ask questions that the other person doesn't want to answer because they may not want to admit out loud what they're experiencing inside. At those times, make sure you show care and concern for the other person's feelings. Unless you're questioning an identified terrorist who's holding back vital information, in which case, go for it!

I was recently working with a client who wants to communicate with clarity, confidence and courage when managing conflict. When I asked her what was important to her, she became very quiet. When I asked her again, she responded, 'Well, you know. . .' and her voice trailed off. Her eyes were moist and her lips were trembling as she looked down at the table between us. I quietly said, 'You seem sad' and she began to cry. She told me about her struggles dealing with conflict, speaking up for herself and how she allows other people to determine her fate while she plays the helpless victim. By my asking insightful questions and addressing what's important to her she is gaining control over her behaviour, acting with authority and demonstrating robustness. By my having asked her challenging questions, demonstrating empathy and respect, and waiting for her to respond rather than allowing her to avoid answering, she is reaching her goal.

When asking questions to gain more information than you've been given, use the word 'exactly' to find out more detail: 'How *exactly* did your ball break the window?' Avoid asking 'why' as that form of questioning is often perceived as threatening and can result in people feeling that they need to justify their actions and becoming defensive in the process.

Respecting people's feelings

Whether you agree with what someone is feeling or not, don't judge. People's feelings come from their personal experiences and though you may struggle to understand how they can feel the way they do, accept that everyone's experience is unique and true for them. When you do, you open the door for unbiased, non-critical and non-judgemental communication. Flip to the earlier section 'Letting go of judgement' for more about this skill.

Respect other people's feelings and you make them feel valued. When people feel that you value them, they're more likely to share information with you that they wouldn't otherwise.

Chapter 5

Establishing Rapport for Effective Communication

I'm sure that you can recall situations when you experienced great rapport with another person; perhaps you refer to those times as being 'in sync' or 'on the same wavelength'. This situation usually occurs when you share similar beliefs, values and interests. The conversation flows easily, you feel understood and you relate well with one another in a relaxed, respectful way.

The *Oxford English Dictionary* defines *rapport* as 'a close and harmonious relationship where there is common understanding'. When you're in rapport with other people, you feel a sense of connectedness and responsiveness based on familiarity and trust, allowing you to establish agreeable relationships with shared understanding. Communication is easy, trust and understanding are paramount, and though you may not agree with the other person's point of view, you can understand their perspective and they can understand yours.

At home and in the workplace, rapport is vital for easier, more straightforward and clearer communication. When you develop rapport with someone they feel that they're being listened to and acknowledged. As a result they tend to focus on common ground and similarities and put differences aside.

Sending and receiving

The word *rapport* derives from the French verb *rapporter,* which translates as 'to bring back' or 'to return'. In simple terms, when applied to relationships, *rapport* means that what one person sends out, the other person returns.

In this chapter I introduce a few methods for establishing rapport so that you can communicate in a winning way, whatever the subject matter and whether you're speaking to work colleagues, strangers or friends.

Building Trust and Camaraderie

Trust, friendliness and mutual support are essential to developing effective rapport. You have to want to establish a relationship with other people, which, as the origin of the word implies (see the nearby sidebar 'Sending and receiving'), is a two-way, back-and-forth process:

- **Demonstrating curiosity in other people:** Their likes and dislikes, beliefs and behaviours, interests and concerns.

- **Being willing to reveal aspects of yourself:** Including your attitudes and assumptions, and acknowledging the impact of your actions.

Pay attention to both sides of a relationship and you're well on your way to building trust and establishing rapport.

Demonstrating curiosity

Eleanor Roosevelt is quoted as saying, 'I think, at a child's birth, if a mother could ask a fairy godmother to endow it with the most useful gift, that gift would be curiosity.' The more curious you are the more you avail yourself of opportunities and possibilities. Your worldview expands as you enhance your level of understanding. You open yourself to learning and engaging with people, places and things, so enriching your life and becoming an interesting person others want to know.

Curious people are often fun to be around and real experts at establishing rapport and building relationships. They're naturally interested in people, and so instead of focusing the conversation on themselves they engage with and learn about others. They come across as enthusiastic, energetic and comfortable with who they are. They ask questions and give you their full attention and because they demonstrate an interest in you, in turn you find them interesting and want to get to know about them. Asking sincere questions (check out the later section 'Finding common points of interest') and really listening to people (as I describe in Chapter 4) leads to rapport and strong relationships.

If you want to find out what makes people tick, ask them. Too often people rely on their assumptions without finding out the facts, which can lead to misunderstandings and a lack of trust (as I discuss in the later section 'Making your assumptions clear'). Showing that you're curious about other people indicates that you care enough about them to want to get to know them and that you're a good listener – one of the most vital components for successful communication (Chapter 4 contains tips and techniques for becoming a first-class listener).

Curiosity is key to great business communication. In business, the best salespeople are curious. The saying 'telling isn't selling' is well known in the sales arena where, all too often, salespeople tend to 'show up and throw up.' Instead of rushing through the sales process, forcing their agenda onto the buyer, the best salespeople demonstrate their curiosity about the environment potential clients are working in as well as the issues they're facing. They seek to understand their clients' concerns so that they can help them achieve their goals. This approach gets people to open up and makes them feel that you care about them personally and that you're not just interested in what you can get from them professionally. As Peter Schutz, former president and CEO of Porsche, once said 'I don't care how much you know until I know how much you care.'

You have two eyes, two ears and one mouth (check in the mirror if you're not sure). Use them in that order and you'll learn more about other people than if you do all the talking.

Here are some benefits of demonstrating curiosity when doing business:

- ✔ Facilitates understanding
- ✔ Promotes trust
- ✔ Increases awareness
- ✔ Can change a main objection into a moderate concern

When you're asking questions of a potential customer, make sure that your questions are open-ended, non-judgemental and non-threatening. Questions that begin with phrases such as 'How can I help you to. . .?', 'Who else needs to. . .?' and 'What do you see as. . . ?' help clarify understanding and demonstrate your interest in the customer's concerns.

A crucial difference exists between being curious and just plain nosy. If you notice that someone's reticent when answering your questions, back off to avoid building a blockade rather than rapport.

Finding common points of interest

Frequently, clients tell me that they feel shy asking other people questions about themselves. They're afraid of coming across as forward and pushy. But when you're genuine about wanting to communicate successfully and establish rapport, all that shyness, introversion and insecurity vanishes as you focus on building trust and camaraderie.

Whether being interviewed for a job or establishing a group of friends when you move to a new town, aim to discover where you share common points of interest. If you want to get to know someone in particular, do some research. For example, in today's world of instant electronic connection, you can look up someone on Facebook or LinkedIn or follow them on Twitter (for more about making the best use of social media, flip to Chapter 12).

Open-ended questions – those typically starting with 'who', 'what', 'where', 'when', 'how', 'tell me about' – are great for discovering shared interests, because they encourage full, meaningful answers that can lead to discovering genuine insights. When you ask people open-ended questions you're inviting them to share their knowledge and feelings, enabling you to find points of commonality in a non-threatening way. In contrast, closed questions, which elicit short, single-word answers such as 'yes' or 'no', can make you sound intrusive and intimidating.

 When you're being interviewed for a job, focus on the interviewers as people who want to engage with you, not as people who are set on making your life as difficult as possible. Visualise them as welcomed guests in your home whom you're glad to see and want to make feel at ease. Set yourself the goal of understanding them and their interests, needs and concerns rather than focusing on how they perceive you. By finding out where you share interests in common, you build rapport by gaining their trust.

Seeking similarities

'Birds of a feather flock together' as the saying goes. In other words, people tend to like people who are similar to themselves. You feel comfortable with people who understand your point of view and have similar experiences and passions. Similarities provide a foundation for establishing rapport.

That's fine, you may think, but what if you have nothing in common with someone? Well, perhaps look a little harder. As long as you believe that there's a bridge that connects everyone, all you have to do is find it and you'll discover similarities between yourself and anyone else that can lead to a productive relationship.

 To establish rapport with someone, aim to emphasise the similarities and minimise the differences between yourselves.

Similarities come in all shapes and sizes including:

- ✔ Background
- ✔ Children and ageing parents
- ✔ Dress and shopping habits
- ✔ Favourite food, play, book, film, sports, holiday destination
- ✔ Political and religious affiliations
- ✔ Schooling

✔ Values and beliefs

✔ Way of speaking and behaving

✔ Where you live

Kathryn and Beth meet at an industry conference. Kathryn is with a group of work colleagues and Beth is running one of the workshops. Because Kathryn's group looks friendly, with the people standing in an open position (see Chapter 8 for more about open positions and rapport), Beth feels comfortable approaching them. The group members welcome her into their conversation and share stories about their experiences at networking events.

Eighteen months later, Kathryn contacts Beth and invites her to pitch for some business for her company. Kathryn tells Beth that she remembers their conversation and Beth's amusing tale of another group that closed ranks when she approached rather than opening up to her. Kathryn relates to Beth's incident because she'd also experienced similar behaviour. As they speak, they share other experiences, including their favourite television programmes, which increases their rapport. When Kathryn suggests that Beth watches a programme that she'd previously disregarded because the title turned her off, she gave it a go, believing that if Kathryn, with whom she already shares similar interests, thinks it's worth watching, she may be interested in watching it too. Discovering that they share similar interests, their rapport builds rapidly and Beth gains a new client. Because their commonality is genuine, Beth and Kathryn's rapport is sincere.

Faking an interest to appear that you've something in common with someone else is a phony pretence that can easily backfire.

Making your assumptions clear

Wherever you are and whatever you're doing, you communicate with other people. Whether you're at work, play or within the family, being open and honest is the best way to communicate. I'm ashamed to admit it but if you're anything like me, you probably make a few assumptions from time to time, despite wanting to do otherwise. Such assumptions can get in the way of rapport, so state your assumptions upfront to ensure that you're reading off the same page as the people you're engaging with. Doing so also allows you to nip in the bud any potential conflicts that may arise.

Instead of acting on your assumptions, confirm them first. For example, if you're new to a team ask how the team members work together. Find out individuals' expectations and working practices. If they're different from what you're used to – in other words, your assumptions – say so. Ask whether your way of doing things is going to fit comfortably with theirs because the way you do things may aid (or indeed damage) your attempt to establish rapport.

Confirm with your colleagues on a regular basis where you stand in relation to your work. Check that you're all in alignment, talking about the same things and working towards the same goals. By stating your assumptions and asking others about theirs, you avoid potential problems and strengthen rapport.

Although you may know what you're talking about, your words can hold different meanings for others. Check with your colleagues, friends and family members to make sure that they understand what you're saying. No matter how straightforward your words sound to you, different people can assume a different meaning, depending on their experiences.

Kristina transfers from the London headquarters of her employer to the New York City office. Kristina is used to the way her London-based team operates and when she arrives in New York, she resolves not to carry any assumptions that may get in the way of establishing rapport and productive working relationships in her new environment.

Annette, Kristina's boss, asks the marketing team to create a report for the senior leadership. Kristina asks Annette to clarify what she means by a draft report, specifically what the report needs to contain. She wants to be clear about the amount of detail to include at the early stage as opposed to later in the process. By checking her assumptions and clarifying the expectations upfront, Kristina ensures that she meets Annette's expectations and works productively to meet the team's deliverables.

Acknowledging the impact of your behaviour

Depending on people's preferred way of communicating, the way you behave can pull them towards you or push them away. (As my son often reminds me, 'one man's ceiling is another man's floor'.) Although a particular way of behaving may be successful when working with my personal assistant, behaving the same way with my financial director can have a negative effect.

When you observe how other people behave you'll notice that some respond well to the stick while others require the carrot; some need care and attention while others prefer to be left alone; and some people's behaviour causes distress, confusion or sadness while others' leads to clarity, happiness and joy. Knowing the impact of your own behaviour determines the kind of rapport that you do (or don't) create.

Behaviour that draws other people towards you includes:

- ✔ Active listening
- ✔ Eye contact
- ✔ Physical touch
- ✔ Reliability
- ✔ Treating people the way they want to be treated

While touching can pull people towards you, the action can push others away. Before touching people, make sure they're comfortable with physical contact and that the contact is appropriate. For example, in Asia, touching people on the head – even children – is considered rude and invasive. People in inferior positions wouldn't touch their boss. Touching someone on a personal part of the body – thighs, for example – sends out sexual messages. In other words, be careful where you touch someone and make sure that person is okay with physical contact!

Behaviour that pushes others away includes:

- ✔ Arrogance
- ✔ Criticism

✔ Dishonesty

✔ Inconsistency

✔ Indifference

Taking the time to identify how people behave gives you an insight into how to act around them. To build rapport with other people, reflect back the behaviour you see them demonstrating (as I describe in the later 'Matching and mirroring posture and energy' section).

Your behaviour shapes the quality of your relationships, so examine and hone your behavioural style to match that of others to enhance your chances of establishing trust and building rapport. By demonstrating flexibility and adapting your style to meet the needs and styles of others, you improve communication, deepen relationships and develop productive connections.

Although identifying the impact of other people's behaviour on you may be fairly straightforward, acknowledging the impact of your behaviour on others and acting on it is more difficult – especially when your behaviour is hurtful or has negative consequences. But persevere because doing so puts you well on your way to building trust and rapport. When others see that you're able to recognise and admit the effect of your actions, they're more likely to want to develop a relationship with you than if you're blind to the consequences of your behaviour, blame others or keep your insights to yourself.

Taking responsibility for your behaviour is a process that involves:

✔ Appreciating how your behaviour affects other people.

✔ Admitting that your behaviour is a result of your specific choices.

✔ Accepting that your behaviour may have negative consequences.

✔ Taking action to repair the harm where possible.

✔ Making changes to avoid similar behaviour in the future.

When you do so you demonstrate accountability. Although taking responsibility for inflicting harm on other people may be a humbling if not painful experience, it shows that you

want to build trust and develop rapport, and that you're
willing to take all the necessary steps to do so.

Engaging with Empathy

In essence, *empathy* is about being able to share other people's
feelings or ideas (and so it's a deeper experience than sympathis-
ing). From my research, I've discovered that empathy covers a
broad spectrum of definitions including but not limited to:

- ✔ Caring about people and wanting to help them.
- ✔ Experiencing similar emotions to those of another person.
- ✔ Knowing what another person is feeling and thinking.

When you demonstrate empathy you gather information
that goes beyond your personal perspective and takes you
into another person's view of the world. Empathy connects
people and binds them together, establishing rapport based
on trust, appreciation and understanding. Sadly, not everyone
can demonstrate empathy, which impacts negatively on their
relationships (see the nearby sidebar 'When narcissism takes
over'). The following sections guide you in how to engage
people with empathy.

When narcissism takes over

Some people lack the ability to
experience empathy and instead
focus on their own sense of personal power, prestige and vanity. As
defined by the American Psychiatric
Association, Narcissistic Personality
Disorder (NPD) causes sufferers to
demonstrate an extreme need for
admiration, an insidious pattern of
pretentiousness and a lack of empathy. They're prone to jealousy, disregarding others' feelings and taking
advantage of other people to reach
their own goals, founded solely on
their own self-interest.

Children naturally go through a
phase of exaggerated self-worth as
part of their development and before
the age of 8 fail to understand the difference between who they are and
their idealised self. Most children
gain better self-understanding later
by comparing themselves to friends
and peers, although those with dys-
functional interactions with parents –
a lack or an excessive amount of
attention – continue to compensate
by seeking to impress others and win
approval while showing no interest
in developing genuine friendships.

Without genuine empathy, your chances of building rapport are nil.

Appealing to people's feelings

My father used to say, 'People buy on feelings and justify with facts.' Making people feel valued is a sure way of building rapport and engaging with empathy. Focusing your attention on what's important to people – demonstrating interest and showing that you care about them and what they're experiencing – takes you a step closer to building a solid foundation for successful communication.

Political speechwriters and advertising executives know how to appeal to people's feelings. They need to generate emotions within people to get them to vote for the politician or buy the advertiser's product. These writers know that people's emotions carry more force than their reason and that appealing to logic on its own seldom spurs people into action.

In *Persuasion & Influence For Dummies* (Wiley) I devote a section to the Ancient Greek philosopher Aristotle's theory of persuasion. Here are some of the emotions to which he says you can appeal:

- ✓ **Anger:** An urge to seek retribution for yourself or your friends. For example, anti-war demonstrators, civil rights campaigners and social activists, who are angry with the status quo, can establish rapport through their shared rage.

- ✓ **Confidence:** The pleasurable anticipation of events, objects or ideas that are favourable to positive outcomes. People tend to accept ideas from those in whom they have trust or confidence. When you demonstrate your expertise and experience, other people believe you and follow your lead.

- ✓ **Fear:** A negative feeling rising from anxiety, dread or a phobia. You can establish rapport by appealing to people's fears. You can rely on a threat to their wellbeing – such as smoking, overeating or hanging out with a bad crowd – to motivate them to take action to prevent something happening that has negative consequences for them.

- ✓ **Love:** Seeking to give the people you care for things that you view as good. Offering words of praise, flattery and approval strokes people's egos and can lead to rapport by making others feel good about themselves.

The heart rules the head

Charities and non-profit organisations are expert at appealing to the feelings of potential donors. Research shows that the most successful approach to take when soliciting funds is to appeal to the heart rather than to the head. Personal stories, focusing on identifiable individuals, generate more donations than dispassionate descriptions of unnamed statistical victims. Perhaps that's why charities employ posters featuring a specific child to raise money for a general cause.

Appealing to people's emotions makes getting them to take action or perform at their best easier than concentrating on logic alone.

Some people are so adept at keeping their emotions under wraps that you may struggle to decipher their emotional state. At these times, pay particular attention to how people are communicating. Noticing physical gestures and facial expressions can tell you more about such individuals' emotional state than the words they say.

Standing in other people's shoes

A traditional saying states that 'you can't really know a man until you walk a mile in his shoes'. It means that you should try to understand people before criticising them (and, fortunately, not that you need to swap footwear!). To establish rapport and engage people with empathy you need to be able to consider things from their points of view, listen to what they have to say without judging or making critical remarks, and allow them their experiences without drawing attention to your own.

Accepting others' emotions

Emotions are tied to people's values and beliefs. Arguing or judging individuals' emotions is both disrespectful and counterproductive. Telling someone that their emotions are foolish, stupid or unsupportable is rude, impertinent and ill-mannered.

Stop and think the next time you're tempted to say something like, 'How can you be so silly?', 'It's not so bad' or 'That's the most ludicrous thing I've ever heard.' People's feelings come from *their* personal experiences, skills and knowledge – not yours – and everyone's truth is true for that person. Although you may struggle to understand how other people can feel the way they do, try to accept that their experiences are different from yours and so are bound to colour their emotions.

The more you're able to open up to your own feelings and neither deny nor distract yourself from them, the more you can accept the feelings of others. *Emotional Intelligence For Dummies* by Steven J. Stein (Wiley) is filled with tips for building your emotional skills.

When you know how another person is feeling, instead of trying to make them feel better or tell them that they're wrong for feeling the way they do, simply accept their emotion. You can respond by telling them that you can see why they're feeling that way and give them time to talk. If you feel comfortable enough with the person, you can offer a sign of affection, such as a hug or a tender touch. Although empathy is usually reserved for accepting people's negative emotions, including pain and sadness, you can also demonstrate empathy in times of joy, accomplishment and success. In that case, a 'high five' may be an appropriate sign of empathy.

Acknowledging people's experiences

Engaging with empathy allows you to demonstrate that you're aware of other people's emotions. When trying to build rapport you can't rely on people telling you how they feel, and so you have to ask them questions, listen for understanding and interpret their non-verbal behaviour. Acknowledging others' experiences means allowing them to tell their tales without you imposing yours.

If you've ever had someone cut in on a story you're telling to top it with one of their own, you know how annoying it can be – it's a sure-fire way to stymie rapport. To avoid indulging in one-upmanship, listen with the intention to understand and acknowledge the other person's experience without interjecting your own story. (You can gain lots of helpful listening tips in Chapter 4.)

Jan is known for her tendency to interject herself into someone else's experience and take over a conversation. One evening, she bumps into Robin and Julia at the pub where they're talking about a concert they recently sang in and where they felt they could have sung better. They want to commiserate and figure out how they can perform better the next time. Uninvited, Jan joins them and begins telling about a concert she sang in where everything went wrong, including her forgetting the lyrics and the pianist playing in the wrong key. Instead of allowing Robin and Julia to get their feelings out and explore their experience, Jan barges into the conversation, relegating the couple and their experience to the sidelines. The next time they see Jan make a beeline for them at the pub, they excuse themselves, saying that they have to talk in private.

Creating Alignment to Build Rapport

Personal alignment is about understanding yourself. When you're in balance with your surroundings, when you act according to your core values and when you can express your values to others, you're well on your way to creating personal alignment. Building on that foundation to create *alignment* (agreement) with others requires you similarly to understand and embrace others' perceptions, qualities, visions and values. When you do so you construct a sense of relatedness and mutual understanding based on similarities, understanding and respect for individuality.

When you're in alignment with other people you're aiming for the same goals and holding similar values. You don't necessarily have to agree with another's point of view although you do respect and appreciate their right to their opinions. You naturally reflect back their body movements, facial expressions and use similar vocabulary. You look the other person in the eye while engaging in conversation, focusing on the impact of your non-verbal behaviour. By demonstrating a willing attitude, comparable values and similar behaviours, you're on your way to building rapport.

In this section you discover how matching other people's behaviour, really listening and leading in a conversation helps to create alignment with others.

Establishing rapport in the workplace

In the world of work, alignment among employees is vital for the success of the business. Without alignment objectives aren't met and goals aren't reached. Examples of poor alignment include:

- ✔ Increased incidences of individuals defending their own interests.

- ✔ Withholding information from peers to make the individual appear more knowledgeable.

- ✔ Complaining about and blaming others.

- ✔ Unsatisfactory implementation and disregard of work commitments.

Follow the tips in this chapter, especially in the next sections, to establish rapport in the workplace.

Matching and mirroring posture and energy

In order to create alignment and establish rapport, practise the technique of mirroring and matching people's behaviour, including the way they position themselves and the energy they emit. Instead of mimicking their behaviour, which would be interpreted as mocking and cause offence, your goal is to move in unison, similar to people dancing, in order that you can tune into how others are feeling, thinking and experiencing their world. By reflecting back the overall tone and demeanour that you observe, you can build a connection and establish similarities. (Check out the earlier section 'Seeking similarities'.)

When you want to establish rapport with someone, notice how they position themselves. Whether their posture is upright and erect or slouched and relaxed, replicate the attitude in your own posture. In addition, note the person's energy levels – are they mellow and laid back or supercharged and animated? – and reflect back what you observe. When you and the other person are in similar physical states you're building rapport, and when you're in rapport, communication flows. *Persuasion & Influence For Dummies* by yours truly (Wiley) contains lots of tips and techniques for mirroring and matching to establish rapport.

When mirroring, be careful not to fall into the trap of parodying the other person's behaviour because they won't trust you and they certainly won't want to engage with you. Instead, act with sincerity and sensitivity to build trust and establish rapport. Also, don't mirror and match other people when, for example, they're experiencing a personal crisis or severe depression or when you want to change the flow of the conversation.

Listening for understanding

The more you discover about other people, the better equipped you are to establish rapport with them. To understand what makes them tick, what turns them off and what matters to them, you need to listen.

Studies demonstrate that people only remember 10–50 per cent of what they hear. Although that's a pretty wide range, the point remains that little of what you say to others, or what they say to you, is remembered. That's unfortunate, but the good news is that listening is a skill that, with desire and practice, you can develop. You can learn not only to hear the words others are saying, but also to understand the complete message that's being sent, including unvoiced thoughts and feelings.

Turn to Chapter 4 for loads more information on developing your listening skills, including paying complete attention, demonstrating that you're listening, providing encouraging feedback, not judging and responding appropriately.

If you find yourself becoming emotional in response to what someone says, let the person know and ask for more information. Certain phrases can go a long way in establishing goodwill and clarifying understanding, such as 'I may not be understanding you correctly' and 'I'm taking your comments personally. I thought I heard you say. . .Is that what you meant?'

Pacing and leading to advance the conversation

When two or more people are interacting, they're consciously or unconsciously influencing each other. If you want to establish rapport to create clear communication, pace your listeners – by matching their external behaviour, including their body language and vocal patterns – to win their trust and attention. When they feel comfortable with you, they'll be willing to let you take the lead.

Pacing means that rather than demanding they understand you, you seek to understand their viewpoints, no matter how strange or off-the-wall they may appear. When you successfully apply matching techniques (see above section, 'Matching and mirroring posture and energy') you're pacing the other person.

When you're pacing people, you're acknowledging them, which in turn builds a bridge of understanding.

Part of pacing involves being aware of and matching other people's vocal patterns and body language that's telling you about their unspoken feelings. (Flip to the earlier section 'Matching and mirroring posture and energy' for more information.) If you want to go into more detail about how to match and pace, pick up a copy of *Neuro-linguistic Programming For Dummies* by Romilla Ready and Kate Burton (Wiley).

The point of pacing is to build a strong connection between you and others to create quality communication. When you've successfully paced other people by approximating their posture, gestures, voice tone and breathing rhythm, you can confidently proceed to lead them in the conversation.

To help you understand the concept of pacing, think of running in a relay team. Only when you're running at the same speed as your team-mate can you successfully pass over the baton. To translate this concept into the context of communication, only when you understand what others are experiencing can you communicate with them successfully and lead them to your way of thinking.

Although pacing involves matching someone until they feel comfortable with you, *leading* is when you slowly – and I mean slowly – start to change what you're doing. If you go too quickly or move too abruptly, you risk breaking rapport, meaning that you have to start all over again.

If you want to see an expert pacing and leading his audience, have a look at Tom Hanks speaking to the Yale graduating class of 2011 (www.youtube.com/watch?v=baIlinqoExQ).

Part III
Putting Your Mind and Body into Your Message

'I blame his Community Skill class
– He filled himself with air, unlocked
his jaw, loosened his lips, let his
tongue move but it all went terrible wrong.'

In this part...

Here's where you get physical and find out how to deliver messages that are clearly thought out and expressed with confidence, conviction and credibility. You discover how to move like you mean it, speak like you care and convey your message in a way that compels your listener to, well, listen.

Chapter 6

Choosing the Right Attitude

* *

In This Chapter

▶ Taking responsibility for your feelings and attitude

▶ Understanding the effect of your attitude on listeners

▶ Connecting effectively with other people

* *

*E*veryone has a 'guiding attitude', which is a way of looking at life that drives your behaviour and determines your way of thinking and feeling. Whether your general attitude is positive, negative or ambivalent, your evaluation of people, objects, events and activities impacts on other people's attitudes towards you. As a result, your attitude determines how successful you are in both your professional and personal lives.

According to the twentieth-century Swiss psychologist, Carl Jung, your personality is set at birth. Your attitudes, on the other hand, are the results of direct encounters or observations and can change depending on your experiences. So although attitudes can have a powerful influence on your behaviour, they aren't set in stone, and certain influences that cause you to have one attitude may, at another time, bring about a change in your outlook. For example, to resolve conflicting inner attitudes about a political issue, you may choose to adhere to one attitude over another.

As international author and achievement guru Brian Tracy says, 'You cannot control what happens to you, but you can control your attitude toward what happens to you, and in that, you will be mastering change rather than allowing it to master you.'

The attitude you send out is likely to be the one you get back.

Watch the way people behave and speak if you want to spot their attitudes. For example, people who show up at work early with smiles on their faces and a readiness to volunteer demonstrate a positive attitude. On the other hand, those who drag themselves into the office late and groan about their workload are communicating a negative attitude.

You may also note that attitudes are infectious. Spend time with someone who's upbeat and you find yourself viewing the world in a positive light. Hang out with people who are down in the dumps and chances are you're going to end up there with them. In this chapter you discover the power of taking responsibility for your own attitudes and behaviours – and their effects on other people – as well as ways of developing a positive mindset.

Speaking from the 1-Position

From time to time you're going to feel threatened, hurt, sad or lonely. As a result you may engage in angry confrontations with family, friends, colleagues and possibly even strangers who cross your path at the wrong time. Along with raised voices and lingering arguments you may start the conversation with statements such as 'You always put your personal interests before company priorities,' 'You're so rude' or 'You never listen to me.' If so, the responses you provoke are probably defensive and hostile rather than open and accepting. The people you're having a go at end up feeling that they're being blamed for your emotions and before you can say 'Bob's your (defensive) uncle', they're coming back at you with fierce denials or counter assaults. Sound familiar?

In this section, you discover how to avoid such escalating tensions by changing your attitude and resulting behaviour and how to speak from the I-position.

Discovering the I-position

In stressful situations, you need to express your thoughts and feelings in a clear, approachable and honest way that the people you're speaking with can understand and respond to positively. Therefore, begin your sentence with 'I feel. . .' rather than 'You should. . .'. In this way, you adopt an attitude that takes responsibility for your own emotions instead of dealing other people the 'You make me feel' guilt-trip card, which is bound to create anger and resentment.

Speaking from the I-position is a non-judgemental way of describing other people's behaviour that's causing you difficulty, without blaming or judging the other person. It consists of four parts: your feelings; the other person's behaviour; how the behaviour connects to your feelings; and what you need to happen. To speak from the I-position, you use I-statements along the following lines:

- ✔ I feel _____(state your feeling)

- ✔ When you _____ (describe the actual behaviour)

- ✔ Because _____ (say how the action connects to your feeling)

- ✔ What I'd like is _____ (recommend action to address the behaviour)

If you're a manager speaking to one of your team members who's not performing up to scratch, you may say:

'I feel anxious when you fail to meet your deadlines because I'm afraid we'll miss our targets, which will threaten all our jobs. For now, what I'd like you to do is to create a progress report that we can review at the end of every week for each project you're working on so that we can monitor your progress and I can provide additional support when you need me to.'

If your boss or partner is a yeller, perhaps you can say:

'I feel offended when you shout at me because I want to be treated with respect. What I'd like from you is for you to speak to me in a calm way so I can take in your message.'

Speaking from the I-position requires a healthy dose of self-disclosure, which can lead you into vulnerable territory. A potential feeling of exposure, however, is worth the discomfort if your words and attitude extinguish arguments rather than fan the flames. When people speak from the I-position they stay more connected than if they revert to name calling – even in emotionally charged encounters.

A benefit of 'I-statements' is that because they focus on your feelings, the other person can't argue or disagree. You're not blaming or holding them accountable for your emotions, you're just telling them how you feel. When you blame people you leave yourself open to disagreement and argument.

By speaking from the I-position you're being clear about your feelings and what you need from the other person.

Using I-statements

I-statements (which I define in the preceding section) form the foundation for co-operative communication by connecting people, building trust and creating healthy, open and honest relationships. When you speak from your own point of view, without assigning blame or foisting responsibility onto others for what you're experiencing, you open the door to candid, productive communication free of fault and judgement.

I-statements build a bridge for communicating when relationships have been soured by squabbles, damaged by distrust or harmed by hurt feelings. They provide information about your feelings in a way that's less threatening than You-statements, which cast aspersions and point the finger of blame. (Later in the 'Appreciating the Power of Your Actions' section, I look at You-statements and the damaging, accusatory language they can cause.)

The following suggestions help you create effective, non-threatening I-statements that demonstrate a positive, constructive attitude:

- ✔ **Be specific:** Saying 'When you ignore me at parties, I feel marginalised' is the pathway to doom. Instead, 'I felt hurt last night when you left me on my own' is specific, direct and communicates your feelings without pointing the finger of blame.

- ✔ **Shun the 'should' and 'ought' words:** When you criticise people by saying 'You should do. . .' or 'You ought to. . .' you're concealing your own feelings about a situation and come across as self-righteous and bossy. Claim your own feelings by phrasing your statement along the lines of 'I feel insecure when you. . .'. By speaking in that way you live in the moment with your feelings and express them without recrimination.

- ✔ **Leave out the labels:** When you call people 'stupid', 'crazy', 'idiot', 'selfish' and other derogatory remarks, you're putting them into negative categories and demonstrating an unconstructive attitude. Instead, comment on your feelings about other people's behaviour, not the people themselves. Seek to understand what compels people to behave the way they do and don't judge them for their actions.

- ✔ **Avoid concealing negative You-statements under the guise of I-statements:** When you say 'I feel that you don't care about me' or 'I feel like I don't matter to you' you're disguising your true feelings about being scared, lonely, hurt or sad by using a veiled You-statement. It's better to say 'I feel unimportant' or 'I feel scared of being alone', for example. Including 'that you' or 'like you' puts the onus onto the other person. (Later in this chapter, 'Appreciating the Power of Your Actions' discusses the negative impact of You-statements, whether they're overtly expressed or disguised as 'I feel. . .' statements.)

- ✔ **Include your feelings:** If you want to establish an emotional connection with people – as the best communicators do – you need to allow them to understand how their behaviour influences your feelings. Camouflaging your emotions creates a false representation of the real you.

Mike and Ian car-pool to work to save on costs. Mike frequently arrives late when he collects Ian, which causes Ian to be late for work and fall behind on his assignments. When Ian's boss begins commenting on his time keeping, Ian knows he has to address the problem. The next time Mike is late, Ian tells him that he feels anxious when Mike collects him after the agreed time because it causes him to be late for his job. Ian says that he needs Mike to be punctual when he's driving so that he can feel confident that he's going to get to work on time and complete his projects on schedule.

By focusing on the issue rather than Mike's personality, Mike thereafter makes a point of arriving at the agreed time. In addition, Ian, who frequently puts others' needs and feelings before his own, understands that his needs are important and expresses them more confidently than before, without nagging, blaming or accusing others (for more on the latter, flip to the later section in this chapter 'Letting go of accusations').

When you speak from the I-position, you're talking about yourself and your own reactions instead of passing judgement on other people. You're compelled to take responsibility for your thoughts and feelings, thus safeguarding others from your accusations, recriminations and criticisms.

You don't always need to start your sentence with 'I' – for example, you can begin by describing the behaviour followed by the effect the behaviour has on you. You then say how you feel about the behaviour and what behaviour you need instead; just ensure that the focus is on how you feel about the situation, instead of how awful the other person is for causing it.

The benefit of I-statements is that the other person can help solve the problem without having to admit culpability. As well as changing the other person's behaviour by pointing out the effect that their behaviour is causing, speaking from the I-position also:

✔ Protects the other person's self-esteem.

✔ Preserves the relationship between you and the other person.

✔ Helps other people understand your reactions and improve their performances.

Speaking from your own point of view

The American clinical psychologist Dr Thomas Gordon helped develop methods for communicating productively and resolving conflicts. Gordon believed that coercive power, in which people threaten or intimidate others to behave against their beliefs and principles, is an inappropriate approach that damages relationships. He advocated active listening (which I cover in Chapter 4) and I-messages. Gordon's methods reached millions of people around the world, including parents, teachers and business leaders, and he's recognised as the originator of a democratic and collaborative leadership model.

Appreciating the Power of Your Actions

You, and only you, are responsible for your actions and your attitude. Although a child can get away with saying 'He made me do it!', when you reach adulthood you're in charge. Despite being easier to hold others responsible for the way you behave, no one can make you act in a way that you don't choose to.

Whatever attitude you bring to the table influences the way you behave and how others respond to you. When you hurl accusations at other people you create a chasm that's hard to cross. In contrast, when you remove the accusations and speak in a way that resonates with your listener, you build a bridge to constructive communication.

Letting go of accusations

People end up feeling defensive and emotionally resistant when you attack them with accusatory statements, especially ones beginning with 'you' (what I call You-statements). For example, if you say, 'You're an idiot,' 'You should be ashamed,' 'You're wrong' or 'You always. . .' the person at the end of your vitriol most likely feels angry, resentful, distrustful or guilty. Don't be surprised if the negative attitude you send out provokes a negative attitude towards you. (In Chapter 2, I address how to remove potential barriers to communication, including casting aside blame.)

Starting a sentence with the word 'you' is bound to lead to trouble because the next words are certain to accuse, criticise or reprimand the person you're speaking to. (For the positive effect of starting sentences with 'I', turn to the earlier section 'Speaking From the I-Position'.)

Sure, the way some people behave can interfere with getting your needs met. A colleague who fails to turn in a report on time, a boss who fails to clarify expectations or a partner who runs up credit-card debt without having the funds to pay the bill can run roughshod over your needs and plans. But telling them that they're responsible for your plight diminishes your power and casts you in the role of victim. Instead, say how their behaviour makes you feel and what you'd like to see them do differently. For example, if your partner enjoys spending money that you don't have, say, 'I feel insecure when you make purchases on our credit card when we don't have the funds to cover the expenditure. I'd like you to discuss with me what you'd like to buy so that we can plan our monthly expenses.'

Cathy is American and her husband, Rolf, is from Germany. Rolf wanted their children to be raised speaking German, even though they live in England. Cathy signed up for German lessons immediately and practised diligently. But when she tried speaking her schoolgirl German to Rolf, he laughed and teased her about her accent and poor grammar. He reverted to speaking to her in English, saying that it was easier. In spite of his criticism, Cathy continued with her lessons and found a German-speaking group in the village to practise with.

She sang her children to sleep with German lullabies and read them simple stories in German. In time, Rolf recognised that Cathy was committed to seeing that their children spoke German, according to his wishes, and began speaking to the children in German as well. Although Cathy often wanted to give up and accuse her husband of not supporting her, she stuck to her promise, maintained a positive and determined attitude and raised two bilingual children.

Them's fighting words!

Research shows that during an argument both men and women experience greater communication satisfaction when their partners use supportive tactics, such as validating the other person's point of view, and less satisfaction when the language is accusatory.

Language moulds people's ways of thinking about problems. For example, when couples are in the midst of divorce proceedings, the focus all too easily shifts to who's right instead of considering what caused the accusations and how the couple and their supporters can improve the way the family functions. Regardless of the circumstances, accusatory language forces people into armed camps, frequently causing emotional damage to those at the receiving end. All too often, people face

disagreement with an automatic, competitive response, looking for what's wrong or weak in someone's position and throwing accusations their way while striving to support their own point of view. Accusatory language is one-dimensional, leads to a lack of interest in how the other person thinks and feels, and prevents you from seeing the bigger picture. Rivals often describe one another in disapproving terms, leaving out or de-emphasising positive attributes.

Instead of taking a position of right/ wrong, good/bad, use the language of compromise to achieve satisfactory results. Sometimes we just have to say, and mean, that while you may not agree on all the issues, you're willing to compromise your position in order to keep the conversation flowing.

Sending a message that resonates

Sometimes you want to make your listeners snap, crackle and pop with excitement, enthusiasm and enchantment when you speak to them. To send a message that resonates with your listeners, you need to know what motivates, inspires and persuades them to engage and listen. To move an audience you have to get in tune with them, to understand their hearts and minds so that you can create a message that links up with their needs and desires.

Some core commitment values

The Core Values of the United States Navy – honour, courage and commitment – set the foundation of trust and leadership within the organisation. Anyone, anywhere, who seeks to live an honourable, courageous and committed life can apply them. Here are the values to sign up to that are relevant to commitment.

'The day-to-day duty is to join together as a team to improve the quality of our work, our people and ourselves, and so I will:

✔ Foster respect up and down the chain of command.

✔ Care for the personal and spiritual wellbeing of my people.

✔ Show respect towards all people without regard to race, religion or gender.

✔ Always strive for positive change and personal improvement.

✔ Exhibit the highest degree of moral character, professional excellence, quality and competence in all that I do.'

Winston Churchill, Martin Luther King Jr and John F. Kennedy were masters at sending messages that resonated with their listeners. Listen to recordings of their great speeches to discover how they tied their personal truths to those of the people they wanted to inspire. They conveyed a clear, compelling message that held a personal meaning for everyone who wanted to turn their vision into reality. Great communicators enthuse and enthral their audiences through their cascading energy. Their messages create a buzzing effect, convincing listeners that what they're hearing is sure to create a better life for them.

Connecting with Commitment

Great communicators know that commitment is key to connecting. Focusing on the other person, respecting individuals and listening with the intention of understanding are all paramount to creating constructive relationships. When you approach communication with an attitude of accepting differences, behaving in a trustworthy manner and responding to other people's needs, you're well on your way to creating clear, committed connections.

In order to connect with commitment you have to:

- ✔ Want to engage with other people, because without that commitment there's no connection.

- ✔ Demonstrate your commitment by speaking with conviction, which means believing in what you're saying and choosing words that express your passion.

- ✔ Tell a compelling story. When you appeal to people's emotions and intellect you're on the path of creating positive attitudes and clear communication.

Wanting to engage with other people

Research shows that from infancy most people want to engage with other people. Sometimes engaging with people similar to you can seem easier than engaging with people who come from different backgrounds, have different experiences or whose values are poles apart from yours. But when you expand your horizons, alter your attitudes and embrace diversity in your relationships, you find that your life is more fulfilling, your opportunities more enriching and your thinking more innovative.

Forming connections with people enhances your perspectives, increases your skills and develops your knowledge. When you connect, any previous negative attitudes you held about them often are transformed and the differences may become the strengths in your relationship.

Engaging with employees

Businesses need to engage with their employees. Research shows that organisations with engaged employees experience increased performance and profitability, which is good news for everyone. To achieve this businesses need to: provide a clear sense of purpose via a strategic vision; engage managers who provide clarity and treat people with respect; encourage employees to voice their opinions; and create a close link between organisational value and behaviours.

Engaging for understanding

When the U.S. Ambassador to India, Timothy J. Roemer arrived in Jammu and Kashmir for a two-day visit in March 2011, he outlined the objectives of his visit: 'I want to engage with the people of Jammu and Kashmir just as I do with the people everywhere else in India. The youth are the leaders of tomorrow who will shape the destiny of the State. I want to talk to them about their hopes and their aspirations for themselves and their community.

I do this everywhere I travel – it is part of my job to talk and listen to people from all walks of life in all regions of the country. I talk to people from all backgrounds and ethnic groups, to better understand the environment I work in and to better perform my job as America's Ambassador to India.' Roemer's attitude of openness and his desire to listen in order to understand are hallmarks of a great diplomat and communicator.

Engaging with others and providing a clear sense of purpose leads to positive outcomes.

Networking effectively

Clients frequently tell me that they find engaging in conversation with people they don't know difficult. The ubiquitous networking events fill them with dread. Reasons including 'I don't know what to say,' 'I feel shy' and 'I feel uncomfortable' are common. If this sounds like you, the best solution is to change your attitude. Instead of focusing on yourself, demonstrate that you're interested in other people. Ask them questions about themselves, their work and their interests. Be open and ready to connect. If you show that you care about someone, that person will care about you.

Here are some tips that may help you to engage with others at one of those networking occasions, when you're feeling shy or unsure:

- **Act like a host.** Treat people with respect and as if they're important. If you're at a networking event, arrive early so that you can greet people as they arrive. Make everyone feel welcome.

✔ **Listen to others with the intent of 'How can I help?'** If you want to be perceived as interesting, show interest. Good things come to those who initiate.

✔ **Give generously.** Great communicators know that exchanging information, making new introductions, sharing contacts, giving referrals and promoting goodwill demonstrate sincerity and lead to new relationships, new opportunities and greater accomplishments.

✔ **Ask for what you want.** People aren't mind-readers. If you don't ask, you don't get – but make requests, not demands. Aim for the long-term relationship.

✔ **End conversations graciously.** Introduce the person you're speaking with to someone else. Give plausible reasons for leaving the conversation. Wanting to make contact with other people is a perfectly acceptable reason for moving to another group, but make sure that you don't just dump the person you've been speaking with.

✔ **Follow through.** Keep your word and foster relationships. If you say you're going to make contact, do!

✔ **Have a clear goal for every event you attend.** Do your homework and ensure that you know who's attending. Ask yourself, 'What do I want to achieve as a result of attending this event?'

Speaking with conviction

In order to speak with conviction you have to care about your subject. When you reveal your passion, believe in what you say and choose words that embrace your message and enhance your meaning, your audience will trust and believe you.

But even with passion, for people to believe in you and in what you say, you need to speak clearly. To start speaking with conviction:

✔ **Articulate:** Pronounce words distinctly and express your thoughts clearly.

✔ **Vary your tone, rhythm, volume and pitch:** To emphasise your points and grab and maintain your listener's interest. Use your voice like a vocal highlighter, emphasising the key words and phrases and injecting variety into the pace and volume.

✔ **Choose decisive language:** To communicate your thoughts and feelings.

In Chapter 7 you can find many vocal tips and techniques for speaking with clarity, composure and conviction.

Indecisive language is a barrier to clear, confident and committed communication. Too many people fill their sentences with fillers – 'er', 'ah' and 'um' – as well as meaningless words that add no substance to their message (see Figure 6-1).

In contrast, decisive language captures your listeners' attention and imagination. Choose action verbs, paint pictures with your words and explain complex issues in simple analogies. For example, when Einstein explained his theory of relativity, he frequently talked about the motion of a man walking on a moving train, which is easier to grasp than 'curved space–time continuum'.

> Y'know...you know what I'm saying...it's so like...okay...like totally not, like, whatever – I'm so not...try...I guess...hopefully...

> I will...We can...I know...Definitely...What I want is...Here and now...I'm convinced... We're passionate... I have a dream...

Figure 6-1: Phrases and sentences filled with meaningless words make you sound inarticulate and lacking in conviction. Decisive language conveys authority, credibility and conviction.

When you speak, speak with your body as well as your words. Look at the people you're speaking to and select your movements, gestures and expressions to support your spoken message. Chapter 8 contains lots more information on conveying meaning through your movements.

Avoid the annoying habit of turning statements into questions. Ending a declarative statement with a rising inflection – as if you're asking a question – is an annoying habit that makes you sound uncertain and causes your listeners to question whether you know what you're talking about.

The American poet and teacher, Taylor Mali, addresses the importance of speaking clearly and with conviction at www. youtube.com/watch?v=SCNIBV87wV4. His message is short, powerful and puts a smile on my face every time I watch and listen.

Telling a compelling story

Well-told stories come from human experiences and resonate with people in a way that dry facts and figures can't. They're dramatic, like cinema and literature, and can change attitudes, beliefs and ideas through narrative, meaning and metaphor. Stories are creative conversions of life's experiences that:

- ✔ Inspire and motivate
- ✔ Train and teach
- ✔ Convince and persuade

If you want to make an idea memorable, tell a compelling story that:

- ✔ Puts your humanity on the line by sharing your vulnerability.
- ✔ Engages, excites and enthuses your listeners by conveying a meaningful message.
- ✔ Creates a physical reaction in your listeners – goose bumps, tingling spines, damp eyes – and a craving to act upon the lessons you share.

Putting together a compelling story

Story-telling is a natural part of the human experience: heroic characters, plot, theme, goal, emotion, action, adversity, climax and resolution. The purpose of a compelling story is to connect and resonate with your listeners, to tap into their hearts and stir their emotions. Bear in mind Aristotle's timeless three-act structure of beginning, middle and end, which is designed to set the scene, create tension and draw a conclusion.

Stories make your message come alive when you tell them with personality, panache and passion.

For someone using a commanding story as part of a presentation, look no further than Steve Jobs launching the iPhone in 2007 (check out this classic at www.youtube.com/watch?v=6uW-E496FXg). Jobs captivates the audience through his 'one big idea' and drives his message home through his passion. He understood that he could tell a story better through showing pictures than by listing words, and he rehearsed like a Broadway star. No secret tricks, magic or mystery: he was simply committed to telling a gripping story that tapped into the minds and hearts of his audience.

If you want to tell a compelling story, live by the following suggestions:

- ✓ **Set the theme:** Make it clear and consistent. When you create a headline that sets the direction for your meeting, you give your audience a reason to listen.

- ✓ **Provide an outline:** Open and close each section of your story with a clear transition. Make it easy for your listeners to listen.

- ✓ **Demonstrate enthusiasm:** Include words such as 'extraordinary', 'amazing', 'cool', 'awesome,' and 'incredible' to wow your audience. Show excitement to share your passion. Sell an experience.

- ✓ **Add analogies to help connect the dots for your audience:** Make numbers and statistics meaningful. Place them in context. For example, when Jobs spoke about his

Macbook Air he said that 4 million had been sold in its first year. Then he broke that figure down into an average of nearly 11,000 per day. That's amazing!

✔ **Make your story visual:** Pictures tell a thousand stories and circumvent the challenges of language. Use as little text as possible. You want to paint a simple picture that doesn't overwhelm your audience.

✔ **Let your inner actor perform:** Embrace the ebbs, flows, themes, transitions and drama of your story. Have fun with flair. Vary your voice and move with purpose. (You can find out more about how to manage your voice in Chapter 7 and your body in Chapter 8.)

✔ **Identify your memorable moment and build to it.** To make story-telling look effortless you have to rehearse: the only secret is to practise, practise, practise.

Add to the drama by saying 'one more thing. . .'. You heighten the excitement *and* make your audience feel as if you've given an added bonus.

Other great examples of superb story-tellers include Steven Spielberg and Nancy Duarte. I highly recommend that you watch their speeches on YouTube to build your speaking skills.

Chapter 7

Speaking with Clarity

. . . .

In This Chapter

▶ Possessing a clear intention

▶ Breathing well to speak well

▶ Using your voice effectively

▶ Selecting powerful words

. . . .

To speak with clarity you first have to be clear in your own mind what you want to communicate. Therefore you need to have a point of view and be willing to share your thoughts, feelings and emotions with other people to get that view across. When you know what you want to communicate to your listener, what you want to achieve as a result of your communication and that you trust yourself enough to show your vulnerability and overcome your insecurities, you're well on your way to speaking with clarity.

Also, ensure that what you say is noteworthy. No doubt at times you've had to listen to someone spew forth meaningless and moronic twaddle in the boardroom – as well as from friends and family – that's meant to pass as insightful and intelligent analysis. You know how frustrating it can be, so ditch the daftness and remember that clarity is power when speaking.

Also, physically speak up. People want to hear what you have to say but if you mumble, stumble and fail to engage with your message, listeners soon lose interest. Speaking with clarity requires that you engage others at the intellectual and emotional levels.

In this chapter I help you clarify your intention and provide techniques for supporting that message with your mind, body and voice. I offer you simple tips for emphasising your points, selecting your statements and engaging with your audience so that they hang on your every word.

Illuminating Your Intention

Having a clear intention, purpose or goal in your mind of what you want to achieve is essential to great communication. But if you fail to communicate that intention in a way that your listener can understand, your efforts are wasted. Having a clear intention *and* communicating it in a way your listener can understand separates a good speaker from a great one. When you connect with and commit to your listeners and add tangible value to their lives, you become a remarkable and memorable communicator.

Misinterpretation and lack of understanding of a message's intention are the main factors that get in the way of effective communication. Yes, speaking loudly enough to be heard and using words your listeners understand are important, but if they don't understand the point of what you're saying, your intention simply isn't going to be received.

As a communicator, your intention is to make the listener understand you.

Great communicators are clear about the impact they want to have on their listeners, whether it's to challenge, excite, inspire, motivate or persuade. Whatever your intention, make sure that it resonates with you. When your intention excites and stimulates you, you can connect with and energise your listeners so that they embrace what you're asking of them.

Clients frequently ask me how they can align their intention with their voice and content. I encourage them to develop an awareness of intention in themselves and others because awareness is key to clear communication. Note the following points to help create a clear intention each time you speak:

✔ **Be honest with yourself.** Notice how you're thinking and feeling, what your attitudes are and what you believe to be true. The thoughts, feelings and attitude you're experiencing translate to your audience. (Turn to Chapter 6 for insights on the power of your attitude.)

✔ **Pay attention to your listeners and ask yourself how they may be thinking and feeling.** What might their attitudes and beliefs be? In addition, ask them how they feel, what's important to them and what their issues are. The more you know about your listeners, the better able you are to align your intention with their concerns.

✔ **Decide what you want to accomplish.** Your intention may be to persuade your listeners to do something or simply to entertain them. You may want to air a grievance or ask a favour. Whatever your reason, write it down and keep that thought in the forefront of your mind as you speak.

✔ **Seek to align your intention with that of your audience.** Work out where your intention and the listeners' purpose for listening intersect and use that as a guideline as you communicate.

✔ **Bring your unique perspective and personality to your speech so that people really hear what you have to say.** When you speak with clarity and confidence, and believe in what you have to say, your audience understands your intention. Later sections in this chapter including 'Supporting Your Breathing', 'Adding Quality to Your Voice' and 'Picking Words That Resonate' are filled with tips for helping you to speak like you mean what you're saying.

To hear someone speak with a clear intention, tune into Dalton Sherman on YouTube (www.youtube.com/watch?v=HAMLOnSNwzA). Dalton is a passionate, self-confident 10-year-old boy whose intention is that individuals work together to make a difference in education. Be prepared to be inspired.

Indirectly speaking

As well as understanding the content (the words) that an individual speaks, effective communication involves understanding the intention (the message) behind the words. Frequently people pepper their sentences with jokes, sarcasm, irony and euphemisms to avoid saying what they really mean. At those times, the content and the intention are at odds. For example, you may have to deliver a harsh message to someone you care about, so rather than coming down forcefully, you may couch your intention in a joke or a euphemism. For example, you might say, 'Good job, not!'. In such cases, successful communication requires that the listener grasps the hidden intention behind the spoken words. For example, if you say, 'John borrowed Louise's idea', the direct word 'borrowed' is code for the intended meaning 'stole'. The statement is designed to play down the wrong, or perhaps through the use of irony to highlight the inappropriate, behaviour.

When determining your intention, keep it clear and simple. Pick action verbs to convey your message and focus on your intention while you're speaking. Ask yourself, 'What's the intention behind my words and actions?'.

If you want more tips and techniques for developing your ability to speak with clarity, pick up a copy of *Voice & Speaking Skills For Dummies* by Judy Apps (Wiley).

Supporting Your Breathing

People judge you not only by your appearance and the words you say, but also on how you sound. Do you speak with authority or is your voice nervy and breathy? Can you be heard at the back of the room or is the front row struggling to catch what you're saying? Proper breathing is the foundation for clear speaking. No matter what the situation – speaking to an audience of thousands or asking your boss for a pay rise – correct breathing relieves nervous energy, helps develop a strong voice and increases personal intensity.

Breathing is automatic and so you probably don't give much thought to how you inhale and exhale, but consider this: without a vigorous circulation of oxygen-rich blood coursing through your body your health is at risk because your tissues atrophy. Without proper breathing your psychological well-being suffers and you can end up with depression, mental dullness or anxiety. Conversely, proper breathing can lead to feelings of pleasure, contentment and mental alertness. Perhaps the time has come to give some thought to how you breathe.

Your breathing impacts on your voice and your voice is a barometer for your mind.

Putting your posture into the picture

Your posture communicates your attitude, thoughts and feelings, and impacts on how clearly you speak. Deep, controlled breathing is a prerequisite for producing a solid sound. The only way you can breathe deeply and in a controlled manner is to position your body in an upright and relaxed posture while filling your lungs with rich, nourishing air. Proper posture (see Figure 7-1), in which every part of your body is aligned with every other part, ensures a deep, rich and resonant voice.

To check that your body is properly aligned, imagine that when standing you can draw a straight line through your ear, shoulder, hip, knee and ankle.

Note from Figure 7-1 that by proper posture I'm not talking about a stiff, rigid, regimental stance in which your shoulders are shoved back, your chin is raised and your chest is thrust forward like the cock of the walk; position your body in this way and you produce a tight, constricted sound. If you force your shoulders back, you tighten up your neck, torso and rib cage, preventing you from breathing deeply and easily.

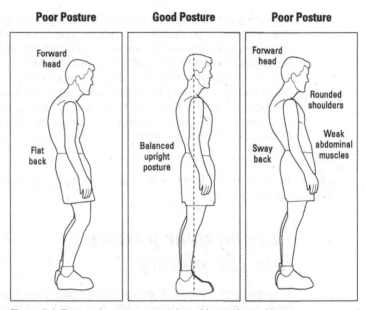

Figure 7-1: Posture impacts on your breathing and speaking.

However, when you sit or stand in a slouched and slumped position, you look like you're uninterested, uninspired and unengaged, and your voice comes out sounding dull, flat and monotonous. Hunched shoulders restrict the expansion of your rib cage, the rise of your diaphragm and the volume of air that can fill your lungs.

Posture and confidence

Researchers have found that posture affects confidence. For example, volunteers who write down their best and worst qualities while seated in erect positions with their chests pushed forward produce significantly greater positive perceptions of themselves than when they're slouched forward with their backs curved. In addition, an expansive, open posture that occupies the surrounding space triggers a sense of power in the mind, making people feel and behave as if they're in charge. Surprisingly, posture contributes more to a person's sense of power than title or position, and so to act in charge adopt a high-power posture.

Practise the following exercise to fill you with focused energy so that you can communicate with clarity, confidence and commitment:

1. **Stand with your feet placed directly under your knees, hips and shoulders.** Imagine that your head is floating on a still lake, with your chin parallel to the ground. Feel your shoulder blades melting down your spinal cord, as your chest softly opens like a well-loved book.

2. **Visualise two streams of energy flowing downwards through the centre of your legs, through the ground beneath you.** The energy is like the deep tap root of an oak tree, keeping you upright and strong.

3. **Imagine that you have shallow roots coming from the bottom of your feet.** They're spreading wide beneath you, making you flexible, like a willow.

4. **Picture your upper body being like a helium balloon, wide, expansive and softly lifting upwards, while your shoulders remain calm and still.** The energy rises through the top of your head, and expands outwards from under your arms and through your back, sides and chest. Hold this position for a count of 20, enjoying the sense of peace and power that comes from proper posture.

When speaking about passion, Isabel Allende describes Sophia Loren – the sexy, slim and tall actress – as a woman who walks elegantly, like a giraffe on the African savannah. When Loren, a woman well into her 70s, was asked how she managed to look so good at her age, she replied, 'Posture and I don't make old people's noises' (www.ted.com/talks/isabel_allende_tells_tales_of_passion.html).

To improve your posture try out some lessons in the Alexander Technique (www.alexandertechnique.com) and/or Pilates classes in your area. Both forms of exercise build abdominal strength, are kind to your joints and lead to proper postural alignment, giving you strength and power.

Filling yourself with air

Breathing is a fully automated unconscious process that begins at birth and ends the day you die. But when you consciously concentrate on your breathing, you can influence and control the flow of air as you inhale for inspiration and exhale for expression.

Two basic types of breathing exist:

- **Chest breathing:** This form of breathing is inefficient, labour-intensive and can make you feel tense, anxious and defensive. Breathing from your chest results in short, shallow and ineffectual breaths, filling only the upper lungs as you hold in your stomach and relying on the muscles in your upper chest, neck and shoulders to draw in air.

- **Abdominal breathing:** When you breathe from your abdomen, like a baby or the family pet, you engage your diaphragm and the intercostal muscles surrounding your rib cage as the lower portions of your lungs take in oxygen. In addition, abdominal breathing is a very effective strategy for reducing stress.

To fill your entire body with life-enhancing oxygen, follow these steps for abdominal breathing:

1. **Place one hand on your abdomen 5 centimetres (2 inches) below your belly button.** Place your other hand on your upper chest.

2. **Inhale slowly and deeply through your nose into the bottom of your lungs.** Note how your abdomen expands, pushing your hand outwards, while the hand on your chest remains still. As long as the hand on your abdomen pushes outwards you can be sure that your diaphragm (see Figure 7-2) is pulling air into the base of your lungs.

3. **Pause for a moment when you've inhaled as fully as you can, keeping your upper chest relaxed and still, and then release the air slowly and fully through your mouth.** Purse your lips and imagine you're blowing on a spoonful of hot soup. As you exhale, release any tension in your body, imagining that your entire

body is loose and limp. As all the air releases, gently contract your abdominal muscles to completely expel any remaining air from your lungs. As you repeat this exercise for a total of five deep breaths, notice that your exhale takes about twice as long as your inhale.

When you breathe deeply from your abdomen, you can relieve nervous energy, develop a strong voice and strengthen personal intensity. Filling yourself with air improves your ability to speak effectively when you're speaking in a stressful situation, such as delivering bad news or asking for a raise.

To develop your breathing techniques further, pick up a copy of *Mindfulness For Dummies* by Shamash Alidina (Wiley).

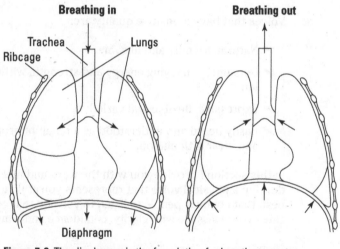

Figure 7-2: The diaphragm is the foundation for breath support.

Adding Quality to Your Voice

Your voice mirrors your personality, indicates how you're feeling now and reflects what you experienced in the past. It's also a gateway (or a barrier) to communicating effectively.

If your voice is squeaky, bombastic, unintelligible, monotonous, mumbled or blocked in your throat people struggle to understand what you're saying and quickly lose interest. If your voice projects cordiality, authority and encouragement, however, you stand a good chance of engaging with your listeners, gaining their respect and establishing rapport with them (flip to Chapter 5 for more on building rapport).

When you want to persuade and influence others, or get them to listen to you with a positive attitude, a quality of friendliness in your tone works wonders. Scolding, snarling or speaking in an unpleasant tone repel your listeners and influence how they view you (which is often badly!). If you tend to speak in harsh and unfriendly tones you may have to review how you view yourself and other people, as well as situations and circumstances in general. For more about using your voice to win over your listeners, check out *Persuasion & Influence For Dummies* by yours truly (Wiley).

Voices that have a positive quality are:

- ✔ Natural, friendly and likeable.
- ✔ Dynamic, conveying energy and strength, without being loud.
- ✔ Expressive, flexible and varied.
- ✔ Easily heard and understood as a result of proper volume and clear articulation.

In this section I provide you with the ways and means to develop a physical voice that represents you at your authentic best, that compels people to listen to you and that communicates your message with clarity, confidence and commitment.

Articulating to be understood

In your haste or hesitancy to communicate you may stumble over your opening words, mumble as you speak or let your voice trail off at the end of your sentences. This is no way to speak with clarity. When you fail to engage your tongue, lips and jaw, expect your listeners to tune out to what you're saying because sloppy speech is too much of a struggle to understand.

Although words are made up of vowels and consonants, the consonants have the power and are key for clear communication. They drive your statements, grab and maintain your listeners' attention, highlight the intensity of your words and stress your emotions.

To increase your expressiveness, clarity and impact, concentrate on accentuating your consonants. In particular, focus on the consonants at the beginnings and ends of your words where they exist. But remember that although clear articulation is vital for making yourself understood, over-articulation takes the feelings out of your words. You want to sound clear, not stilted.

When you want to make a word or an idea stand out, lengthen the consonant at the beginning of the word or syllable you want to emphasise. By stretching the consonant and delaying the rest of the word, you let your listener know that the word you're saying is important.

Studies show that precise articulation is essential for increasing employee productivity, customer confidence and effective presentations.

The primary cause of negative voice quality is tension, emotional as well as physical. When you're able to let go of tension, you're on the way to producing a rich, clear sound.

Lie on your back with your knees bent at a 90-degree angle, your feet together, flat on the floor, and your eyes closed. Notice how your body feels as you breathe in. If you detect any tension in your body, eliminate it by 'breathing into' that area. Breathe deeply to increase your lung capacity. The goal is to relax areas of your body that affect your voice, including your jaw, neck, shoulders, chest, upper and lower back and diaphragm.

Unlocking your jaw

When you lock or tighten your jaw the sound you produce is restricted. A relaxed jaw enhances your speech and enables you to articulate your words and release your voice.

To release your jaw, open your mouth as wide as possible – as if you were about to yawn – and move your jaw sideways, up and down and in circles. Then make wide chewing motions – as if you're chomping on a piece of sticky toffee – while humming gently. Repeat five times.

Excellent emphasis

Dr Martin Luther King Jr's 'I Have a Dream' is one of the world's most outstanding pieces of oratory, not only because of its historical context but also because of his use of emphasis throughout the speech. You can read Dr King's speech at many Internet sites and watch his delivery on YouTube. Five forms of emphasis that make this speech so powerful are:

Anaphora, a rhetorical device in which Dr King repeats words at the beginning of neighbouring clauses. By repeating the words twice he sets a pattern, which further repetitions emphasise, and so increases the rhetorical effect.

Repetition of key theme. He voices the following words repeatedly throughout the speech: 'freedom', 'we', 'our', 'you', 'nation', 'America', 'American', 'justice', 'injustice' and 'dream'.

Fitting quotations or references. For example, Biblical allusions serve as a moral basis for King's arguments as does his reference to the Declaration of Independence.

Examples to illustrate his arguments. He gives his speech meaningful geographical reference points by referring to specific states and areas within the US.

Metaphors to highlight contrasting concepts. By using metaphors he associates the concepts in his speech to concrete images and emotions.

Loosening your lips

Although a stiff upper lip helps you hold back emotion, it hinders clear articulation. To loosen your lips practise the following exercises five times at least once a day:

- ✔ **Make a sound like a motor boat or a horse's blow,** by placing your lips loosely together and exhaling in such a way that the air passes between your lips causing them to flap. Allow the spittle to fly!

- ✔ **Spread your lips in a smile** saying 'eeeee', open them and say 'aaahh' and then close them and say 'ooooo'. Repeat five times.

- ✔ **Say 'pit-pat-pit-pat-pit-pat-pit-pat-pit-pat' five times,** pronouncing the 'Ps' and 'Ts' clearly. Repeat, increasing the speed. Make sure you enunciate the 'Ps' and the 'Ts'.

✔ **Repeat the following phrases five times.** Start off slowly and build up gradually until you can say them at normal conversational speed. When speaking these tongue twisters, exaggerate the words, making your tongue, lips and jaw work:

- Rubber baby buggy bumpers

- Five fresh fish specials daily

- Six stick shifts stuck shut

Moving your tongue

If your tongue is taut or flops around in your mouth like a wet fish, you strain to speak clearly. Tease your tongue and release tension by repeating the following exercises five times:

✔ Double your tongue back against your palate as far as you can and then stretch it outward from your mouth as far as possible.

✔ Push your tongue hard against one cheek and then the other. Lick your lips in a circular fashion over the upper lip and down over the lower lip. Then waggle your tongue from side to side.

✔ Round your lips tightly then groove your tongue and push it through the opening.

✔ Press the upper surface of your tongue against your palate and release. Repeat, increasing the speed of the motion.

Emphasising your points

Emphasis is the force or stress you place on selected words or phrases to highlight ideas, concepts and feelings. When you use vocal emphasis, you're letting your listeners know that what you're saying is important, which encourages them to pay attention.

Although words convey meanings, the particular meanings come from the way you emphasise or express them. You can change the meaning of a simple sentence just by emphasising different words. For example, say the following sentence, emphasising the italicised words each time and note the different meanings that are conveyed according to which word you stress:

 ✔ *Lianne* must go to Paris.

 ✔ Lianne *must* go to Paris.

 ✔ Lianne must *go* to Paris.

 ✔ Lianne must go to *Paris*.

Pitching

To add colour and excitement to your speech, add inflection by altering the pitch of your voice. When you're excited let the sound reverberate out of the top of your head. When you're sharing your feelings, speak from your heart. If you want to sound like an authority, let your voice resonate from your chest, bouncing off your sternum. And when you want to convey the wisdom of the ages, drop your voice to deep within your body.

If your volume is too loud you may come across as sounding aggressive, defiant and angry. Conversely, if your voice is too soft, you can sound bored, tired or shy.

Pacing

To keep your listeners engaged, vary your pace. When you change the ideas, meaning and the emotions you're conveying, your voice naturally slows down or speeds up. Whatever you do, avoid the monotone. Like the sound of a cruising aeroplane engine, a monotone is a sure way to put your listener to sleep.

Speaking too quickly makes you sound nervous but speaking too slowly makes you sound dim. Instead of focusing on your speed, concentrate on the intensity of your message (I address intention earlier in the 'Illuminating Your Intention' section).

Pausing

When you want to separate ideas and hold your listeners' attention . . . pause. That moment of silence between words and phrases lets your listener know that something important is about to happen. Pausing gives you the opportunity to catch up with yourself and listeners the chance to absorb what you've said.

Picking Words That Resonate

The words you speak impact on the way others perceive you. Great speakers know that their message needs to resound and ring true in order to connect with their listeners, command their attention and compel them to listen. Your words need to be relevant to your listeners' experience, contain force and energy, be clear and concise and lead from one thought to the next.

Adding gusto and passion

If you want to excite, enthuse and engage your listeners, inject some fervour into your language. If you speak in a lacklustre, wearisome and humdrum way, don't be surprised if you fail to inspire, motivate or influence your listeners. When you appeal to your listeners' needs and concerns and address your remarks to their fears and anxieties, you can arouse their enthusiasm and excitement.

In 1933 when US President Franklin D. Roosevelt said in his first inaugural address, 'The only thing we have to fear is fear itself,' the depression had reached its lowest point. People were jobless, homeless and struggling to survive. By outlining in broad terms how he planned to govern and reminding his countrymen that America's 'common difficulties' concerned 'only material things', he brought hope to a crippled country by acting on his spoken promises, demonstrating strength and leadership.

For further examples of talks that carry gusto and passion review the speeches of Barack Obama, Mother Teresa, John F. Kennedy, Anita Roddick and Dr Martin Luther King Jr.

Let go of hesitant and wishy-washy language by dropping words such as 'try', 'maybe', 'hopefully' and 'sort of', because they carry no vigour, weight or authority. Replace them with words like 'we will', 'our aim is to', and 'when' (rather than 'if').

Sticking to the rule of three

Pick up a book of fairy tales, ancient myths or some of the world's great stories and you can find the number *three* popping up in some fashion on a regular basis: *The Three Musketeers,* 'Faith, Hope and Charity' or 'Friends. Romans. Countrymen'. Humans need to process information in patterns and because three is the smallest number of components required to form a model, a pattern based on this number can help you create a message that is bold, brief and easy to remember (see, three things).

Three points in a pattern pull people in because you've condensed your message to its essence, cutting out the clutter.

Cutting through the clutter

If you want people to listen to what you have to say, get to the heart of the matter: drop the blah, blah, blah; let go of the mumbo-jumbo; ditch the jibber-jabber.

When you speak, keep your message simple:

- ✔ Stick to strong verbs and precise nouns to express facts.
- ✔ Pick verbs that pack a punch to motivate, inspire and command your listeners' attention.
- ✔ Limit your use of adverbs and adjectives, which fill your sentences with personal opinions that your listeners can nit-pick and argue with.

As Leonardo da Vinci said, 'Simplicity is the ultimate sophistication.'

Bridging to stay on track

When you want to focus and remind people where you are in the discussion, build a bridge to take you from one thought to the next. Like an arrow on a map saying 'you are here', bridges take you from where you are in the conversation to where you want to go next.

As a speaker you're responsible for guiding your listener from one thought to the next. Bridges form useful transitions that relate one fact to another, creating a smooth flow of thoughts instead of bombarding your listeners with a load of unrelated information they struggle to make sense of. In addition to helping your listener stay on track, building bridges creates trust; they're more willing to let you guide them through your speech. When they trust you they relax, and when they relax they're more open to being influenced by what you say.

Bridging techniques can be divided into two categories: four techniques that *pull* your listener along and three that *push*. Here are the four pulling techniques, starting with the most popular:

- **Transition words or phrases:** These include 'firstly', 'next', 'finally', 'also', 'in contrast to', 'equally important', 'on the other hand', 'speaking of which', 'for example', 'in addition to', 'as well as', 'which is why', 'even so' and 'then there's always'.

- **Silence:** If you make a thought-provoking point, you need to give your listeners time to absorb, reflect and then move on. A silent transition can be powerful (see the earlier section 'Emphasising your points' for more about the power of the pause).

- **Movement:** Dipping your head, making a gesture or moving from one spot to the next emphasises that you're making a transition. Be careful not to make too many movements if you're speaking in Asian countries, where listeners tend to be more interested in what you have to say than in 'show business' (flip to Chapter 11 for communicating across cultures).

- **Internal summaries:** When you're offering a lot of information, take care to remind your listeners of the points you've covered before moving onto the next. When you say phrases such as, 'So, what we've looked at so far is', 'You've seen how' or 'Now, let's look where this logically takes us', you provide a sense of order and pattern.

The following three transitions that push your message along set up an expectation for the audience for what's coming next:

✔ **Visual aids:** When you provide your listener with something to look at, you create expectations. Steve Jobs was a master at showing his audience the latest iPhones and iPads, keeping his listeners engaged and excited.

✔ **Rhetorical questions:** When you ask a question, your audience expects you to provide the answer. This technique moves your listeners to the next point.

✔ **Sequencing:** Tell your listeners that you're covering three points and they feel a sense of comfort, knowing that you're organised (read the sidebar 'Sticking to the rule of three' for why you use three points).

Chapter 8

Conveying Messages through Movements

. . . .

In This Chapter

▶ Communicating moods and feelings with your body

▶ Engaging others with facial expressions

▶ Understanding and using body positions to communicate

. . . .

As the American dancer Martha Graham stated, 'The body says what words cannot.' The way you deliver your message – including gestures, expressions and posture – adds meaning to the words you speak. Between 50 and 80 per cent of all human communication is non-verbal, because your gestures, movements and expressions, combined with your vocal quality, reveal your attitudes, emotions and those sentiments you may want to leave unspoken. (Read more about using the voice in Chapter 7.)

Although some of your body language is conscious, many of your movements aren't. The more mindful you are about how you manage your body language to convey your messages, the better you can communicate with clarity and precision. Equally, the more adept you are at interpreting the movements of other people, the more insight you have into their unspoken attitudes and feelings.

In this chapter I give you insight into using your stance, gestures and facial expressions to support your spoken message or to convey your meaning when words escape you.

Letting Your Body Do the Talking

Although you need words to convey factual data, how you express your message through your bodily movements – including gestures and posture – influences how others receive and interpret the meaning behind the message. Some movements even have linguistic translations, such as waving your hand instead of calling out 'hello' in the US or 'no' in much of Europe, nodding your head in agreement or shaking it when you're in dispute. Many gestures are widely understood, although they may carry different meanings in different cultures. Check out Chapter 11 for how to avoid non-verbal pitfalls in foreign lands.

When you smile at people, lean forward towards them and look them in the eye, your non-verbal behaviour is helping you to establish and maintain relationships. When you avoid eye contact, frown more than smile and physically pull away from people, you're indicating that you're not interested in engaging with them. To persuade individuals to your way of thinking, use non-verbal messages such as an upright posture and a steady gaze to demonstrate your self-confidence and conviction.

Discovering the five silent emotional displays

Kinesics is the study of communication through body movements, facial expressions and gestures. The term refers to the way different human gestures reflect feelings and attitudes and was developed in the 1950s by anthropologist Dr Ray L. Birdwhistell. Although an obvious form of non-verbal behaviour, kinesics can be confusing because various meanings are communicated through the same movements across different races and cultures. (Read more about communication differences across cultures in Chapter 11.) For now, however, consider that throughout your day you use five different kinds of kinesics as you communicate with friends and family, strangers and colleagues, as well as your boss and peers:

✓ **Adaptors:** You use adaptors as a means of satisfying a personal need, such as scratching to relieve an itch or pushing your hair out of your eyes. Adaptors also relieve tension. When you're feeling uneasy or anxious you may fidget, play with objects, adjust your clothes, bite your nails, tap your desk, fiddle with your hair, tap your legs or rub your nose. As well as indicating that you're feeling nervous or upset these nervous habits or involuntary ticks can even make you appear preoccupied, fearful or dishonest.

✓ **Affect displays:** These facial expressions and body movements convey feelings and emotions. These actions suggest whether someone is open and receptive, tense and closed, annoyed, upset, distracted or any number of different emotions. Many affect displays are commonly interpreted, such as individuals sitting in a slumped position with frowns on their faces appearing dejected or uninterested and people staring at each other with tight lips, clenched hands and deep frowns as feeling hostile towards one another. In contrast, those sitting upright, smiling and with wide open eyes and raised eyebrows can be seen as engaged and cheerful.

Sometimes the affect displays you observe may not be related to the interaction you and another person are having. For example, if the individual you're engaging with has a splitting headache, he may squint, look down, rest his head in his hands and grimace during your conversation. You may think that he disagrees with you whereas in fact he's simply indicating that he's in pain.

✓ **Emblems:** When you want to substitute a gesture for words or phrases, you use emblems. A beckoning index finger is saying 'come here' and a forward-facing waving palm is a way of offering a greeting, but an open hand held upright and still means 'stop'. Be wary of emblems; what's acceptable and friendly in one country is obscene and insulting in another, as I describe in Chapter 11.

✓ **Illustrators:** Frequently you use movements that illustrate the words you're saying to support or reinforce your verbal message, including the shape and size of an object you're describing. For example, while saying 'yes' or 'no' you may nod your head in agreement, or shake your head in disagreement. You may rub your stomach when you're hungry, shake your fists when angry and gesture towards the right when you're referring to something in that direction.

Be careful with interpreting illustrators, because although they're more universal than other gestures they're still open to misinterpretation. For example, men and women often interpret the simple nod differently, with men indicating that they understand what they're hearing, whereas women nod in accord.

✔ **Regulators:** These gestures monitor, co-ordinate, maintain or control the pace and flow of conversation. When you want to finish a formal meeting you may stand up, push away from your desk, look at your watch or put your pen in your pocket. If you're speaking with someone at a party and want the conversation to end, you may turn your head and start to move away. Often, when people are uninterested they look at the floor, ceiling or any place other than at the speaker.

Regulators let people know when you want to speak, when you want them to speak or when you don't want to speak. For example, when you want to speak you may lean forward and open your mouth. You nod your head in an individual's direction when you want that person to speak. When you don't want to speak, you may simply close your mouth, shake your head and look downwards.

In order to avoid misinterpreting the kinesics you observe, note the following three basic rules:

✔ **Always read gestures in clusters:** Clusters are similar to verbal sentences, in that to understand the message you need to hear and observe more than just one word or gesture. To interpret correctly the feelings and attitudes that people are conveying, pay attention to all the gestures and movements on display.

✔ **Look for congruence:** When someone's words match his gestures, expressions and movements, that person is in a state of congruence. If you want to be clear about someone's state of mind, observe the gesture clusters and how congruent they are with the words being spoken. (For more about how congruence influences meaning, pick up a copy of *Coaching with NLP For Dummies* by Kate Burton (Wiley)).

✔ **Consider the context:** The environment can influence the gestures on display. For example, most people behave quite differently at a formal dinner with people of high authority than at a barbecue with a group of young children.

Bringing your body into play

Two basic groups of body language postures exist:

✔ **Open or Closed:** This posture is the easiest one to spot. When people fold their arms, cross their legs and turn their bodies away from you, they're signalling that they reject what you're saying. When people show open hands, face you fully and plant both feet on the ground, they're accepting what you're saying.

✔ **Forward or Back:** This posture indicates whether people are actively or passively responding to the communication. When people lean forward in your direction, they're actively accepting or rejecting your message. If they lean back, gaze upwards, doodle, polish their glasses or fiddle with their smartphones, they're passively absorbing or ignoring what's being communicated.

In combination, the two postures form four different modes (as the following four sections and Figure 8-1 show), which help us to recognise the 'hidden' messages of non-verbal communication.

Figure 8-1: Posture groups in combination create four basic modes: responsive(Open/Forward), reflective(Open/Back), fugitive(Closed/Back) and combative(Closed/Forward).

Responsive mode (Open/Forward)

When individuals are feeling responsive their bodies indicate that they're actively accepting. If you're doing business with someone whose body is in this position, you want to close the sale, ask for agreement or request a concession.

Here's what to watch for:

✔ **Engagement:** Body position open and leaning forward with palms showing.

✔ **Eagerness:** Legs open, feet under the chair with the weight on the toes, body leaning forward.

✔ **Readiness:** Puts down pen, gathers papers together, places hands flat on the table.

Now's the time to pull out the contract to sign.

Reflective mode (Open/Back)

When people are in the reflective mode they're interested and receptive but not ready to commit. At this point you want to present more facts and offer incentives, and also give them some quiet time so they can consider what they've heard.

Watch out for:

✔ **Listening:** Head tilted and frequently nodding, lots of eye contact, a high blink rate.

✔ **Evaluating:** Chin-stroking, sucking on pencil or glasses, eyes focusing upward to the right.

✔ **Attentive (standing position):** Feet in open position, smiling, hands possibly behind back.

Fugitive mode (Closed/Back)

You can spot people in the fugitive mode because they attempt to escape the room physically or fade mentally into boredom. At this point you want to spark their interest in whatever way you can (short of shouting 'Fire!', that is).

Notice the following:

✔ **Defensiveness (standing position):** Feet pointing inward, closed fists.

✔ **Boredom:** Gazing into space, slumped posture, doodling, tapping feet.

✔ **Get me out of here:** Feet pointing towards door, looking around the room, buttoning jacket/coat.

✔ **Rejection:** Backwards movement, folded arms, crossed legs, frowning, head down.

Combative mode (Closed/Forward)

People in this mode demonstrate active resistance. At this point you want to defuse any anger, avoid contradicting, steer away from arguments and guide the other person into the reflective mode.

Here are the relevant signs:

✔ **It's my turn:** Finger and foot tapping, staring into space, lip chewing or tight mouth.

✔ **Aggressiveness:** Leaning forwards, pointing finger, clenched fists.

✔ **Defiance (standing):** Hands on hips, frowning, down-ward-turning mouth.

✔ **Lying:** Face touching, hand covering mouth, ear pulling, shifting position, looking upwards to the right, which is where the eyes tend to focus when the brain is imagining or creating.

Looking to the right can also indicate that the person doesn't know the answer and is guessing, speculating or talking hypothetically. For more about eye movement and meanings, pick up a copy of *Neuro-linguistic Programming For Dummies* by Romilla Ready and Kate Burton (Wiley).

To signify an open attitude in a business environment, unbutton your suit jacket in front of the prospect. This gesture indicates that you're willing to negotiate. Removing your jacket is a sign that you want to establish a closer rapport with someone, and when you roll up your shirt sleeves you're showing that you're ready to get down to business. Politicians frequently remove their jackets and roll up their shirt sleeves as a means of showing that they're just like their constituents.

If non-verbal behaviour holds particular fascination for you, pick up a copy of my book *Body Language For Dummies* (Wiley), which covers the subject from top to toe.

Putting Your Face into Your Message

Whether you're smiling, sneering, grimacing or frowning, more than any other part of your body your face conveys how you feel about what you're experiencing. This fact holds true whether you're from an Asian, a Western or any other culture. Research dating from the 1800s to the modern day consistently shows that certain facial expressions of emotions are unequivocally universal.

From childhood onwards you find out how to conceal certain emotions and emphasise others through specific facial management techniques. In addition, you discover rules about the appropriateness of displaying emotions. For example, if someone you don't like receives bad news, instead of dancing with joy as you celebrate the other person's misfortune, you put on a sad countenance to demonstrate your feigned distress. Violate this rule at your peril, because to do so makes you appear insensitive.

Here are some facial management techniques to practise on a daily basis:

✓ **Intensifying:** Intensifying or exaggerating facial expressions shows the strength of an emotion. For example, if you win an award you probably intensify your positive expression by smiling more broadly than usual and raising your eyebrows.

✓ **De-intensifying:** You de-intensify or underplay your expression when you want to subdue an emotion, such as covering up your own enthusiasm when you're in the company of a friend or colleague who didn't receive the same good news as you.

✓ **Neutralising:** At times you want to avoid showing any facial expression, such as when you're being reprimanded in public or feeling sad and want to keep your emotions to yourself.

✔ **Masking:** When you want to hide your true feelings you may put on a false face, perhaps when you want to curry favour with your manager despite being given an onerous task. Instead of showing how you really feel about the assignment, you mask your feelings by adopting a happy face.

Becoming adept at managing your facial expressions helps you to interact with your boss, colleagues and clients with enthusiasm, confidence and in an appropriate manner.

According to extensive research, if you tune your antennae you can interpret accurately six basic human emotions through facial and eye expressions, no matter where you are in the world. When you don't speak the same language, your ability to read signs and signals can make you friends and keep you out of trouble. Here are the identified expressions and signs to watch for (see also Figure 8-2):

✔ **Anger:** The eyes narrow and the eyebrows lower and pull together in the centre of the forehead as the lips tighten over the teeth. If the teeth are exposed, the mouth takes on a rectangular shape. The jaw is tightly clenched and the lower jaw may jut forward.

✔ **Disgust:** The muscles around the nose activate and the eyes are more relaxed than when someone is angry. The eyebrows lower as the upper lip raises. The signs may appear only on one side of the face.

✔ **Fear:** The eyes widen in a frozen stare as the upper eyelids rise. You may notice sweat on the face as well. The eyebrows draw together and the lips open.

✔ **Happiness:** The key visual component to happiness is the smile, in which the corners of the mouth lift. In addition, the eyelids tighten, the cheeks pull up and the outside corners of the eyebrows pull down in a genuine smile.

Within the mammal population, only humans bare their teeth when smiling, because in the animal kingdom bared teeth is an aggressive facial sign.

✔ **Sadness:** The eyes gaze downwards and to the side. The eyebrows are arched outwards, the head bows or tilts forward, and the mouth turns down at the sides, sometimes slightly open and trembling.

✔ **Surprise:** The eyebrows lift in a curve while horizontal lines cross the forehead. The upper eyelids stretch open and the lower lids come down. The jaw drops, the lips and teeth part and the effect is of a slack jaw.

When someone's surprised, if the head is forward it indicates disbelief. If the head is pulled back, it indicates fear.

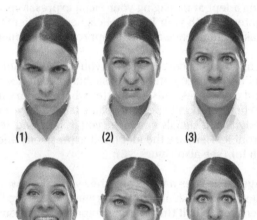

(1)   (2)   (3)

(4)   (5)   (6)

Figure 8-2: The six basic human emotions: anger (1), disgust (2), fear (3), happiness (4), sadness (5) and surprise (6).

 Facial movements on their own communicate basic human emotions. When combined with other forms of body language, such as posture, unconscious physical movements and deliberate gestures, you can decipher the intensity of the emotion.

Engaging with your eyes

Although you've undoubtedly heard this expression before, I include it as a reminder: 'The eyes are the mirror of the soul.' Your eyes are a means of communicating and indicate whether or not you're receptive to what someone has to say. Depending on the amount of time you hold someone's gaze, you demonstrate how much interest you feel for an individual, if any at all.

How and when to make eye contact depends on the customs of the culture, who you're with and the social setting you find yourself in. In some cultures you're considered aggressive, disrespectful and ill-mannered if you look another person in the eye, whereas in others you're perceived as rude if you don't. For example, in many Asian cultures, avoiding eye contact with someone of the opposite sex or in a superior position is a sign of respect, but in the US and most of Europe eye contact is a necessary component for establishing yourself as a confident and engaged individual. In addition, maintaining eye contact demonstrates power at home as well as at work. When you communicate with people in Eastern Europe, including former Soviet countries, eye contact is the norm. If you have to communicate through an interpreter, maintain eye contact with the top person as a sign of respect. In Muslim countries, men and women avoid eye contact, although prolonged eye contact between men demonstrates respect and loyalty. (See Chapter 11 for more about cultural differences.)

Amala is a corporate lawyer in a London law firm. Her Asian background meant that she used to struggle to make eye contact with the firm's partners, most of whom are male, because in her culture eye contact with superiors is considered a sign of disrespect. Although the partners were impressed with Amala's work and her ability to establish rapport with clients and colleagues, they perceived her lack of eye contact as a sign of weakness, insecurity and shyness, none of which was true. Amala knew that in order to be promoted to partner, she had to change her superiors' view of her and that one way of accomplishing this was to look them in the eye when answering their questions and offering her opinion. Breaking the rules of her culture was a challenge that required a lot of practice and a clear view of what she wanted to accomplish. Amala still finds looking her male superiors directly in the eye uncomfortable, but she doesn't let that prevent her from doing so and was recently promoted to partner.

Eye contact regulates conversation and gives clues of dominance. When you look people in the eye you can pick up signs about their attitudes and thoughts. The familiar expressions in the following list indicate just how much information and meaning can be communicated through the eyes:

- ✔ She looked daggers at him.
- ✔ He had a gleam in his eye.
- ✔ She has doe eyes.
- ✔ He has shifty eyes.
- ✔ She gave him the evil eye.
- ✔ If looks could kill.

Whether people have Bette Davis eyes, Spanish eyes, bedroom eyes, sad, defiant or piercing eyes, they're revealing their moods, attitudes, feelings and points of view.

Avoid staring or having a fixed gaze unless you want to make someone feel uncomfortable. Look directly into the other person's eyes for 3–5 seconds, before breaking eye contact to show interest, self-confidence and that you're paying attention. Blinking normally, nodding or shifting your head during a conversation demonstrates that you're engaged and comfortable. Blinking rapidly and frequently reflects nervousness or discomfort. Repeatedly looking away or refusing to make eye contact can be interpreted as weakness, lack of interest or disrespect.

Moving your mouth

In addition to communicating through the spoken word, your mouth can convey subtle messages, revealing your thoughts and feelings without you uttering a syllable. For example, as an infant you use your mouth to suckle at your mother's breast or on the teat of a bottle, which is a calming and pleasurable experience. As you mature, this comforting and nurturing action connects psychologically to feelings of love, happiness, security and sex, so don't be surprised if you find yourself licking your lips when you're feeling sexually aroused or enjoying moments of joy and satisfaction.

Table 8-1 contains a substantial list of mouth movements and the messages they convey.

Table 8-1	What Your Mouth May Be Conveying	
Mouth Position	**Possible Meaning/s**	**Further Explanation**
Glued-on smile	Forced agreement or displeasure	Appears quickly and lasts longer than a genuine smile; the eyes are unengaged
Closed-mouth smile	Secrecy or with-holding emotion	The lips are stretched across the face in a straight line, concealing the teeth, indicating that the person smiling is holding back information
Twisted smile	Mixed emotions or sarcasm	Opposite emotions are showing on either side of the mouth
Dropped-jaw smile	Surprise or false smile	The jaw is dropped lower than in a normal smile while the eyes remain unengaged
Tilted-head smile	Playful, flirting, coy	Head tilted to the side and downwards, partly hiding the face; lips are closed; smile is transmitted to the intended target through the eyes
Biting lips	Tension, worry, anxiety	High levels of concentration
Grinding teeth	Tension, restraint	Suppressing another reaction, including annoyance, fear or anger
Chewing pen or pencil	Self-comforting	Like any sucking action, including smoking and thumb-sucking, this is a self-comforting impulse that relates back to breast feeding
Pursing lips	Thoughtfulness, or upset	Suppressing the words in the mouth until you're ready to release them; can also indicate annoyance or impatience at not being able to speak as well as indicating upset, as if suppressing crying

(continued)

Table 8-1 *(continued)*

Mouth Position	Possible Meaning/s	Further Explanation
Tongue poke	Disapproval, rejection	The tongue thrusts forward briefly and slightly at the centre of the mouth as if tasting something foul; the gesture may be quite subtle but a more extreme version can include a nose wrinkle and squinting eyes
Clamping hand/s over mouth	Suppression, holding back, shock	Prevents you from speaking, perhaps from shock, embarrassment or upset, or for tactical reasons
Nail-biting	Frustration, suppression	A comforting gesture, frequently prompted by fear, anxiety or frustration

Positioning Your Body for Best Effect

To stand, to sit or simply to lie down (the latter isn't recommended during business meetings!)? To lean forward or pull away; to touch or not to touch? These are the questions. Like the words you speak and the gestures you make, how you use the space around you communicates your thoughts and attitudes. Standing close to your listener with your hands on the other person's shoulders, looking him directly in the eye, says something quite different than if you position yourself in a distant corner with your arms wrapped around your waist and your eyes cast downwards.

Proxemics – the use of space – is a way of measuring the effect of space on interpersonal communication and how it varies between cultures and the environment you're in. According to the concept's creator, Edward T. Hall, four different spaces surround a person and indicate the relationship between you and others within these areas. Figure 8-3 illustrates these distances, which are defined as follows:

- ✔ **Intimate:** This area is reserved for the closest contact between yourself and others. Here you embrace, touch, kiss and whisper. Because the space is so small, most people refrain from entering it in public.

- ✔ **Personal:** This 'personal bubble' is kept for good friends and family members and keeps you protected from people you want to hold at a slight distance. This is where most of your interpersonal actions take place.

- ✔ **Social:** When you're interacting at a social gathering, you put yourself in the social area that's reserved for acquaintances and impersonal business. The more distance you put between yourself and others, the more formal the interaction becomes.

- ✔ **Public:** When you're addressing a group at a public event you normally speak from this protective space. From here you can take defensive action if you're threatened. For example, if someone appears menacing, you may keep yourself at this distance, where you can see what's happening but not be close enough to be directly harmed.

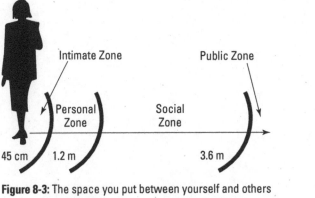

Figure 8-3: The space you put between yourself and others defines your relationship with them.

If you're of equal status to a business associate, you can comfortably reduce the space between yourselves. When the status is unequal, the person holding the higher position may approach the lower-status person more closely than the lower-status person would approach the person with the higher status. If you're conducting business in northern Europe or North America, stand farther apart from the person you're engaging with than if you're speaking with someone from southern Europe or the Middle East, where people stand much closer. (See Chapter 11 for more about what to expect when communicating across cultures.)

Part IV
Managing Communication Challenges

'OK — look out for emotional triggers.'

Part IV

Managing

Communication

Challenges

1n this part...

*1*n this part I let you in on the secrets of communicating
in tough times through developing solid, trusting relationships and having a clear picture of what you want to
achieve. I give you the inside track on defusing tricky situations, avoiding complications and treating other people
the way they want to be treated.

Chapter 9

Getting Yourself Out of Sticky Situations

* *

In This Chapter

▶ Defusing conflict diplomatically

▶ Tackling difficult behaviour

* *

I'm sure that from time to time you find yourself in sticky encounters, and you know just how awkward and uncomfortable they can make you feel. I'm not talking about battling a melting toffee apple at the fairground, unpleasant though that is! I mean those quarrels involving other people when perhaps you say the wrong thing at the wrong moment, feel berated by a dissatisfied client or need to deal with a bullying colleague.

Unfortunately, such difficult situations are part of life, and so you need an emergency kitbag of approaches to draw from when the going gets rough. To help, I provide you with simple tips for handling conflict, managing difficult behaviour and so keeping yourself out of the communication quicksand.

Dealing with Conflict

Communication experts agree on two things: conflict is a result of conflicting values (I discuss the central importance of personal and corporate values in Chapter 5) and it's a normal part of everyday life. When you handle and manage conflict effectively, you can:

✔ **Increase morale.** Both at home and at work conflict can lead to bad feelings and damage relationships. Managing conflict before it gets to the point of no return signals that you care about the other person, which leads to improved relationships and increased self-esteem for all involved.

✔ **Improve social cohesion.** The people in conflict gain a sense of working together to achieve a shared vision. Differences are appreciated as they shed light on all sides of the problem and positive relationships are established.

✔ **Make better decisions.** Conflicts force the parties to look at what's working and what isn't. By gaining input from everyone involved you can come up with alternative solutions, better options and satisfactory resolutions – people feeling satisfied that their contribution led to a positive result.

✔ **Stimulate innovation.** Research shows that collaboration built on a framework of trust adds value by helping organisations achieve superior performance. Collaboration can only be achieved with personal commitment, which can lead to healthy argument and debate. When you're free to test your views against others without personalising ideas, everyone's suggestions can be voiced, leading to quality ideas.

Dealing successfully with conflict is about taking personal responsibility for addressing the problem, and protecting the relationship.

In this section I show you how to defuse conflict before potential issues become major obstacles, so that your communication and relationships can move on. Practising these suggestions and learning from each experience ensures that the next time you find yourself in the middle of a conflict, you have the ways and means of dealing with it in a manner that ensures everyone comes out a winner.

For a more detailed guide to handling conflict effectively, pick up a copy of *Conflict Resolution at Work For Dummies* by Vivian Scott (Wiley).

Seeking to understand other people

Crucial to your efforts to avoid and, if necessary, handle conflict is accepting that other people have their own points of view and respecting those differences. If you can appreciate varying values, expectations and perspectives, and develop the ability constantly to refine and check your understanding of others, you're sure to find that your personal and business lives become easier and more pleasurable.

Asking questions to check your understanding

Conflict comes in many forms and from various sources. Sometimes it arises as a result of poor communication: people fail to say what they mean or they state what they mean in such a way that those listening struggle to understand or accept. At other times, conflict results from the honest mistakes and misunderstandings that arise every day.

Whether the conflict surrounds a teenager's curfew, an employee's duties or an international dispute, asking questions allows you to help prevent the situation escalating into a full-blown argument. As you gather information about the situation, you may find that the facts you have are not the same as those that the person you're talking to has, leading each of you to see the same situation differently.

 Check that you and the person you're in conflict with have the same understanding of the situation; make sure that the information you need to confirm understanding is thorough, complete and objective.

Questions such as 'What were you thinking of?' or 'Why did you do that?' can sometimes sound like perceived assumptions or judgements, which can cause people to respond defensively. To avoid this from happening to you, follow these guidelines for asking questions:

✔ Ask yourself 'What's my reason for asking this question?' to ensure that you're genuinely interested in the other person's answer or perspective, as opposed to challenging or pointing out flaws in the person's reasoning or behaviour.

✔ Let the other person know your reason for asking the question. If people know what prompted you to ask, or your reasons for needing more information about their opinion, they're likely to want to co-operate with you.

Gaining as many bias-free facts as you can helps both parties see the conflict more clearly and can lead to a mutually satisfying resolution.

✔ Use open-ended questions (starting 'what', 'where', 'who', 'how', 'when') to encourage other people to respond in their own words, but try to avoid 'why' questions because they can cause a negative or defensive response.

When you replace judgement with curiosity, you discover new perspectives and possible solutions that you may not have considered before.

Analysing expectations

Disregarding or ignoring people's expectations is a very common reason for conflict. When expectations aren't met or something happens that people didn't anticipate, ineptness takes over and work becomes bungled; along with this come anger, frustration and flare-ups about unrelated views and situations.

Regarding conflict as a situation of differing expectations, instead of a question of right and wrong, allows you to reach a shared understanding.

When you don't get something you were expecting, you can feel disappointed, hurt or angry. If you find yourself becoming negative and closed, stand back and reassess with the other person what happened. Then explore both of your expectations. By working together to uncover what occurred, you can avoid a major row.

When your expectations aren't met, ask yourself the following questions to help you analyse what may have gone wrong and to prepare for making things right in the future:

✔ Was the other person aware of my expectations?

✔ What were the other person's expectations?

✔ Did the other person have the power/authority to meet my expectations?

> ✔ Was it in the other person's best interest to meet my expectations?
>
> ✔ What is the other person's understanding of my expectations?

Recognising different perspectives

Different perceptions and personalities can lead to conflict. When you see things one way and someone else sees them differently, you need to make an effort to understand the other person's point of view and help them to understand yours in order to avoid becoming derailed.

The most effective way to recognise different perspectives is to ask people for theirs, and then listen respectfully with the intention of understanding. When you listen with respect, you demonstrate that you value the relationship and that you're willing to do whatever it takes to settle the conflict. Turn to Chapter 4 if you want to brush up on your listening skills.

Treat others with respect, no matter how much their perspectives differ from yours. By avoiding disrespectful words and actions you can resolve the problem faster than if you judge, criticise or condemn the other person's values and beliefs. In some cases it can prevent conflict from occurring in the first place.

Taking practical action

In this section I offer you practical tips for dealing with conflicts, such as not underestimating the role of emotions and working to defuse a problem rather than fanning the flames.

Watching for emotional triggers

Emotional needs, including love, status, recognition and belonging, often act as triggers that exacerbate disputes. Protracted international conflicts, those between racial groups and ones connected to different life choices, stem from deep-seated emotions. The same is true for spats in the office or tiffs at home.

Suppressed emotions can get in the way of clear communication. Anger, excitement and the fear of seeming foolish or losing face can result in unintended conflict. When you acknowledge emotions, you can communicate your needs without threatening, frightening or punishing others.

The importance of emotions

Emotions are ever-present, potent and can be hard to handle. Along with the power of reason, emotions influence how people evaluate situations and events and can work for or against them. According to Professor Daniel L. Shapiro, Associate Director of the Harvard Negotiation Project, handled wisely, emotions play a part in helping opposing parties reach shared goals. People want to be treated with respect and when they are, they're inclined to work productively to settle a dispute. Even if the dispute can't be settled there and then, by treating one another with respect the parties walk away with the feeling that they can work together effectively and will be able to reach an agreement in time. ositive emotions foster problem solving, open the door for creative thinking and promote empathy between individuals. Negative emotions are linked to erroneous judgements and a lack of concern for what matters to others.

When disputes arise, remember that emotions play a major role in the outcome.

An example of this is during the Camp David negotiations facilitated by President Jimmy Carter, when a stalemate between Israeli Prime Minister Menachem Begin and Egyptian President Anwar Sadat almost derailed the process. Begin stuck firmly to his pledge that he'd never allow the dismantling of Israeli settlements and withdrew from the talks. Before he left, he asked Carter to sign a copy of a photograph of himself, Carter and Sadat together for his grandchildren. Carter signed eight photos – one for each grandchild – with a personal message to each. Begin was so moved by this act of kindness that he re-entered the negotiations, leading to a compromise on the settlement issue. By appealing to Begin's emotions, Carter was able to achieve a successful outcome.

Here are some ways of managing emotional triggers:

- ✔ **Recognise and respect your and the other person's emotions.** Try to understand the unexpressed feelings beneath the words.

- ✔ **Clarify the source of the feelings.** For example, anger and distrust can be caused by something that happened in the past, which has nothing to do with what's going on in the present.

- ✔ **Express your feelings in a non-confrontational way.** When you use 'I' messages, you explain your feelings without accusing anyone else. Check out Chapter 6 for further insights into speaking from the 'I' position.

✔ **Acknowledge other people's feelings as legitimate.** Just because they feel differently to you doesn't mean that their feelings aren't real and valid. When you and the people you're in conflict with release feelings, you can deal with the more important issues. Chapter 4 contains tips on listening with the intention to understand.

✔ **Don't react emotionally to emotional outbursts.** If you're struggling to remain calm, call for a timeout and leave the room for an agreed time. Removing yourself from the scene of an outburst gives you time to think and calm down.

✔ **Call for a mediator.** If you can't resolve the conflict on your own, ask someone else to act as a mediator. Finding someone impartial is paramount, so that all parties feel acknowledged and respected. Sometimes professional mediators are required, such as in business cases or divorces, while in other situations a trusted colleague or respected adviser can do the job.

Controlling the situation

If you want to take control of a difficult situation, begin by controlling your own behaviour. When you focus on the way you're thinking and behaving, you may influence the way others deal with you. Similarly, when you control your thoughts you're more likely to produce a positive outcome than if you let your ideas and emotions run wild.

Therefore, keep calm, remain non-defensive and treat others with respect. Let go of any resentment and anger. When you speak, avoid getting angry and speak from your own point of view to eliminate any chance of the other person getting defensive (Chapter 6 has tips on how to do this).

Making the conflict personal is a sure way of escalating the problem. Letting your emotions and personal feelings about the other person get tangled up in the controversy doesn't do anyone any good, even when someone is disagreeing with or attacking your position.

Keeping a cool head allows you more easily to interpret the non-verbal behaviours and hear the messages behind the spoken words than if you're blowing off steam and bombarding others with vitriol.

As one who's had my fair share of conflicts, I know how challenging this piece of advice is. But I'm also well aware from experience that when I present the facts in a cool, simple and unambiguous way, people listen and are prepared to accept what's expected and find the way forward.

Some practical steps for controlling the situation include:

✔ **Decide when to confront the other person (if at all).** You may decide that the issue isn't important enough to you to discuss it or that you'd rather give in this time in the interest of the long-term relationship. When you recognise that you have a choice as to how you're going to deal with the situation, you put yourself in the driver's seat.

✔ **Visualise how you want the situation and the conversation you're having to be, in order to create a positive picture.** See yourself dealing with the situation successfully, speaking clearly, comfortably and confidently. Avoid imagining negativity because this reduces your power in creating a positive outcome.

✔ **Look at the situation objectively.** Put yourself in the other person's position to see the situation from their point of view. Don't deal with the issue if you're feeling angry or excessively emotional.

✔ **Examine the concerns of the other person.** Pose questions (along the lines I discuss in the earlier section 'Asking questions to check your understanding') to find out how the other person feels and sees the situation. Treating other people with respect allows them more easily to replicate your behaviour.

✔ **Consider other options.** Call in a mediator, separate the parties, change the location of the discussion and make efforts to signal empathy by listening without forming judgements and using empathetic body language, such as nodding, leaning forward and keeping your gestures and expressions open. (You can find out how body language helps defuse tension in Chapter 8.)

Part of controlling a situation is to take responsibility for the process and be prepared to resolve the dispute. Seek compromise and avoid punishing. Remember that resolving the conflict is more important than winning or 'being right'.

If you're wrong, admit it. Hanging onto your position for the sake of wanting to be right is a waste of time and makes you look foolish. By allowing yourself to be wrong you show that your interests lie in doing the best for everyone concerned and that you genuinely want to reach a resolution.

When you demonstrate your integrity you show that what matters to you is finding the best result, even if that means relinquishing what you thought was right.

De-escalating the conflict

Everyone involved in the conflict has the right to be treated with respect and consideration. By asserting that right you can focus on the facts and keep things simple. If you allow exaggerations, embellishments and personalities to enter the discussion, you exacerbate the problem.

Focus on issues and not on personality. Calling other people 'stupid', 'thick', 'unfeeling' or any other negative comment escalates the conflict (surprise, surprise!). Instead, encourage them to express their feelings and frustrations, assuring them that they won't be interrupted. Then, follow through on that promise.

Ask what's important to the other person about the outcome and what needs are being threatened. By showing that you care enough to consider the other person's needs and issues you take a giant leap towards de-escalating the conflict.

Perhaps suggest that the individuals involved in the conflict brainstorm possible solutions to resolve it. When you come to a viable strategy, agree on an action plan. Confirm who's going to do what, by when and how. Monitor progress and agree to regular reviews. After the conflict is resolved, move on, and make sure that no one, including you, holds onto old issues.

Managing Difficult Behaviour

Managing difficult people – or better said, people whose behaviour is difficult – is a challenge that expends your time, energy and other resources. Being able to deal with awkward, contrary, demanding or stubborn behaviour effectively and encourage the person who's throwing the spanner in the works to behave in a co-operative and productive way is one of the greatest skills that you can have whether you're a manager, a parent, a teacher or just someone who wants to live a peaceful life.

Wherever you go you're going to encounter people whose behaviour is difficult to manage. For example, they may fail to keep commitments, constantly find fault, don't know when to stop talking, compete for power and refuse to see other people's points of view. No matter what the situation, you have to find a way to address and deal with such behaviour. Otherwise, it simmers beneath the surface and finally erupts counterproductively. For example, if you constantly complain about a colleague's behaviour, you can come off behaving in a difficult way yourself.

Following the suggestions in this section allows you to create a template for managing difficult behaviour and creating positive outcomes.

Treating people with respect

When dealing with difficult behaviour, show people consideration and acknowledge their feelings. When you demonstrate respect and empathy, you accept what the person is saying and experiencing. Your message is 'I understand.' You don't have to agree with people or accept the behaviour; just show that you understand how they're feeling.

When you treat people with respect, you can develop rapport and produce outstanding results. Check out Chapter 5 for ways of engaging with empathy and developing rapport.

Showing that you care about people

If you ask people why they're behaving in a difficult way, usually you receive a flat denial. From their point of view they're not being difficult and are affronted when you suggest otherwise. Instead of getting into a slanging match, show that you care about them by demonstrating patience and listening with an open mind. Although you don't have to like their attitude or their behaviour, caring about them as an individual makes them feel valued and legitimate. Doing so, and displaying an interest in their problem, can lead to people becoming more reasonable in their behaviour.

Tell yourself that the other person doesn't mean to act in a difficult way and make a real effort in your mind to separate the behaviour from the person. When others sense that you're supportive and are willing to listen, they're more inclined to build a positive relationship with you than if you chide and castigate them without hearing them out.

Demonstrating that you care about people doesn't mean letting them off the hook every time they mess up. Point out how their behaviour impacts on the outcome and help them find other ways of acting.

Recognising people's value

Without doubt, valuing someone who's behaving in a problematic way can be challenging. But when you recognise people's potential and the value that they bring to the organisation, team or department, you're well on your way to changing that behaviour.

Look beyond the behaviour and aim to connect with the person as an individual with a contribution to make. People who behave in a difficult way frequently suffer from lack of confidence or low self-esteem. Acknowledge their strengths and positive qualities to let them know that they matter.

Take time to show how much you value people by acknowledging the contributions they make. Doing so may require that you focus on the people's positive qualities at a time when you're ready to knock their block off, but demonstrating appreciation for what they do opens the door for you to show them how they can do even better.

Focusing on behaviour

When dealing with people who're causing difficulties, remain respectful of them as a person and focus on their behaviour and not their personal traits. In particular, avoid using the word 'attitude'. If you tell people that they have a bad attitude, you'd better take a step backwards and watch the barriers to productive communication rise. Instead, give examples of where they responded poorly to task requests, such as, say, consistently turning in reports late.

Keeping the focus on behaviour gives the person who's acting in a difficult manner something to aim for. If you define the problem as the person, you create anger and resentment because people can't change their personalities. If you define the problem as behaviour, you open the door for improvement.

Don't point out unacceptable behaviour in front of an audience of peers or whenever you're likely to cause embarrassment and humiliation. Instead, meet with the person one-to-one and discuss the behaviour and the differences you want to see.

Taking practical action

Confronting people head-on rarely solves the problem of difficult behaviour or defuses the situation. Instead, you need to adopt a positive approach in order not to become part of the problem yourself.

Concentrating on required outcomes

When dealing with difficult behaviour, concentrate on achieving outcomes, such as the goals that define the organisation. These goals can work towards Key Performance Indicators (KPIs), agreed, quantifiable measurements that reflect the success of an organisation. For example, meeting or increasing the percentage of customer calls answered within the agreed timeframe or the number of customer complaints successfully handled. By doing so you empower individuals to contribute to the company's reason for existence. Instead of just doing tasks for the sake of keeping busy, focus on desired outcomes and agreed goals.

Remind the people who behave counterproductively that their behaviour is having a negative impact on reaching the organisation's desired goals. Make sure that you let them know what outcomes you envision, not just the tasks that are necessary to achieve them. By addressing the big picture and how their behaviour can either help or hinder achieving organisational goals, you give them a chance to adapt their behaviour and contribute to the success of the organisation.

To get the best results from people, tap into their internal motivation. Ask them what results they'd like to see, how they'd like to contribute or what suggestions they have for improving their performance. When you ask them the implied question, 'What's in it for me?' you give them the chance to validate their reasons for actively participating, or to clarify why they're not behaving in a productive way.

Keeping your commitments

When dealing with someone whose behaviour you find difficult, you need to stay true to your word. If you make a promise, deliver. Honouring your undertakings shows that people can trust you to make good on what you said you'd do.

Keeping to your commitments is one way of gaining the other person's trust and helps to build a healthy relationship.

Being open and honest

Explain to the person in question how their problem behaviour is impacting on you, your team or the department. If you're unhappy with their behaviour, say so. You can ask them what they want you to change and then let them know what changes you want from them to improve the relationship.

Preferably, talk to the other person face to face and look them in the eye as you say what needs to be said. Speak assertively, making your statements clear with no room for misinterpretation.

Going for the win–win

Forcing people to change causes them to resist and resent you, and they often simply become more motivated to defend their position. Instead, look for a solution where you *and* the other person benefit.

I recently attended a workshop focusing on dealing with difficult behaviour. The trainer asked us to separate into pairs, with one person being A and the other B. A made a tight fist and B was to get A to open it up. The Bs who physically forced A's hand had no success but those who offered an inducement for the As to open their hands succeeded. In that case, both A and B got what they wanted. In one pairing, B told A that she noticed he was carrying a lot of tension in his neck and shoulders and that she was a qualified masseuse. When A admitted that he was feeling tense, B asked if he'd like a neck and shoulder rub. When A said, "Yes," B offered on the condition that A open his fist. By offering an inducement that was more appealing than maintaining a closed fist, A was willing to change his behaviour.

Sticking to the point

Getting sidetracked is all too easy when you're dealing with someone who's behaving in a problematic manner. Name-calling and referring to past behaviours have a way of popping into your conversation, taking you away from the issue at hand. Instead of engaging in mudslinging, take a deep breath and stick to the point. Often when people see that they can't rile you up or change the topic, they tend to relent a bit.

If the situation looks like it's getting out of control, interrupt the person immediately. Suggest you take a break and meet up later. Distancing yourselves from the problem helps calm things down and gives you both the chance to think and reflect on what happened.

Chapter 10

Negotiating with Finesse

● ●

In This Chapter

▶ Planning thoroughly

▶ Starting your negotiations

▶ Going for a win–win outcome

▶ Concluding discussions

● ●

ccording to Roger Fisher and William Ury from the Harvard Negotiation Project, 'negotiation is a basic means of getting what you want from others.' Negotiation is a process, not the end itself. Whether you want your children to eat their vegetables and brush their teeth, to encourage a neighbour to cut their hedges or to convince your boss you're due for a raise, how you achieve your desired outcome is what negotiation is all about.

Not a day goes by when you don't negotiate for something. Whether you're bargaining for limited resources at work, seeking help from people over whom you hold no authority or haggling at the local flea market for a neglected treasure, brushing up on your win–win negotiation skills is a great idea.

The success (or otherwise) of a negotiation depends on two key factors:

✔ **Quality of your relationship with the other party:** How you get on with the other party impacts on how well the negotiation goes.

✔ **Quality of the communication that takes place:** Open and honest communication usually leads to a satisfactory outcome, whereas poor communication is a recipe for disaster.

If you're never going to see the person you're negotiating with again, go right ahead and play hard ball, the game where you try to win and others lose. If, however, you work with the parties routinely, you're better off negotiating with trust, honesty and openness, aiming for an outcome in which everyone involved comes out a winner.

In this chapter I offer you simple tips for conducting successful negotiations, including preparing thoroughly, starting on the right foot, maintaining focus during discussions and finishing up in style.

Preparing to Negotiate: The Basics

Negotiating is an unusual activity in that it's a collaborative effort with inherent opposing views. Therefore, the best way to manage the differences is to be prepared and know your strengths and what's important to you and your counterpart.

Establishing your uniqueness

In today's world of newer-faster-better, being unique is your first port of call when setting out your negotiation strategy. Differentiating yourself from your competitors adds value to your offering by making whatever you're suggesting appear rare, distinctive and one of a kind.

Think of the late Steve Jobs and the uniqueness of his products and the success he had getting the buying public to shell out their hard-earned money. When you demonstrate that your proposition is exclusive, has a special quality or is in short supply, people are more likely to grab your bait than if you're offering the 'same old same old'. Examples may be offering a product or service in a limited timeframe ('You have only one more day to sign up for this seminar at the discounted price') and encouraging your children to do something they may not want to do ('If you eat your vegetables you get to choose which film we watch tonight.')

If you want further information about the value of uniqueness when negotiating, pick up a copy of my book *Persuasion &*

Influence For Dummies (Wiley), which is filled with tips for highlighting the uniqueness of a proposition.

Gaining commitment in principle

When people make a commitment they often feel pressure from within themselves as well as from the people with whom they interact to behave consistently with what they said they'd do.

Therefore, before beginning the formal part of the negotiation process, make sure that you gain a commitment that you and the other person both want a mutually satisfying result. Don't get drawn into negotiating before you gain an agreement in principle to do business together. If you do, you can end up conceding ground before you get to the heart of the matter, giving your counterpart a better starting point.

If you're not sure whether the other person is committed to working with you, ask: 'If you and I can agree on the details, are you willing to go ahead with the discussion?'

Aiming high

Through my own experience as well as in-depth research, I discovered that aiming high when negotiating leads to better outcomes than settling for the lowest common denominator. The principle makes sense: if you aspire to less, you get less, and vice versa.

When you set high aspirations be ready to work hard, prepare carefully and be persistent in your efforts to achieve your goal. Be clear about your goal and don't specify fall-back positions upfront. Whatever you say and do before you begin negotiating influences the expectations and final aim of the other party.

When preparing for your negotiation, determine for yourself your highest justifiable price. Don't tell other people what your final price is upfront because they may be willing to offer more. By price, I mean more than money – for example, you may want a certain amount of time off, flexible working hours, a corner office and so on. As long as you can argue your point convincingly, aim high.

Don't make any ultimatums. Take-it-or-leave-it offers usually end up with you gaining nothing and looking at the other person walking out the door.

Setting Out Your Stall

Reputations are made or broken in negotiations. By getting off to the right start, being clear about your own goals and knowing in advance your and the other side's needs and concerns, you're more likely to gain a successful result.

Letting the other side go first

Encourage your counterpart to go first and patiently listen, never interrupting. The old saying that whoever mentions numbers first loses isn't always true, but you're better off sitting tight and listening attentively instead of showing your hand too soon. Even if the other side doesn't mention numbers, you get the chance to ask what they're thinking.

Alternatively, you can aim for an agreement with your counterpart as to how best to approach the negotiation discussion. Setting ground rules can really help to build trust, but make sure you don't impose them on the other person – ensure there is genuine agreement.

If you're not sure how to start the ball rolling, perhaps say something along the lines of, 'You're more experienced than I am in negotiating these sorts of transactions. What's the going rate? What do you think is fair?'

You can also turn the discussion into an offer by probing the other person's thoughts and fleshing out the details of what they're saying. Then you can paraphrase what your counterpart says as a proposal along the lines of, 'So, from what I've heard you say, you're willing to offer. . .'.

Listing all your requirements upfront

Surprises have no place in a negotiation strategy. If you try to slip in a previously unmentioned requirement just as you're about to sign a contract, you end up looking dodgy, deceitful and devious. Even if your intentions are honourable and you simply forget to include a requirement, you look unprepared and unprofessional.

In addition to laying your cards on the table from the start, confirm the other person's shopping list, too. Everything that's part of or related to the transaction has value, even if you can't put a price tag on it. The other person's needs, including personal, political and emotional requirements, affect the deal. Being clear about such aspects allows you to appreciate the consequences, costs and perceived value of the transaction.

Discover everything that the other side wants before you begin negotiating. Finding out bit by bit wastes time and money. When you negotiate each issue one at a time you have to give and take on each point. By knowing the other party's position in advance, you can look at them as a whole and negotiate accordingly. (Check out the later section 'Keeping the big picture in mind' for more details.)

Defining clear goals

When you and the person you're negotiating with agree that the time has come to buckle up and get down to business, write out a list of goals you want to achieve. I can hear you saying, 'Well, that's pretty obvious,' but you'd be surprised how many people fail to take this simple, orderly step.

Studies show that people who set clear goals achieve more favourable outcomes than those who go into a negotiation with none. Only by knowing what your goals are can you expect to achieve them. After identifying your goals, you can then mull over any fall-back positions you're willing to consider.

Staying Focused During the Process

Having prepared well and kicked off the negotiations effectively (as I cover in the earlier sections 'Preparing to Negotiate: The Basics' and 'Setting Out Your Stall', respectively), you don't want to blow the good start by letting things slip during the heat of the discussion. Follow the guidelines and tips in this section to make sure that the negotiations proceed as you hope.

Being prepared to trade concessions

In order to achieve a successful negotiation in which you and the other party walk away feeling good about the outcome, you both have to be prepared to concede some 'like-to-haves' in order to gain the 'must-haves'. The following tactics can help you achieve a satisfactory result:

- ✓ **Determine and agree all the points for negotiation before getting down to business.** Ensure that you decide whether each point is fixed or flexible.

- ✓ **Make sure that you have plenty of points for negotiation.** The more you know about the other person's requirements, the more positions you have to bargain around.

- ✓ **Trade concessions, don't give anything away.** Every time you make a concession, you want the other person to return the favour. Preface your concession by saying, 'If I offer you this, what can you offer me in return?' Trading concessions builds a framework for reaching agreements.

- ✓ **Offer concessions gradually and in small portions.** Aim to hold something in reserve and when you offer it, do so in a way that lets the other person know it has huge value to you, highlighting its features and benefits.

- ✓ **Ensure that your concessions really count.** People place a high value on what they fight to achieve and are emotionally satisfied when they feel that they've negotiated well.

Keeping the big picture in mind

If you fail to focus on the big picture you can easily get caught up in fighting for relatively unimportant points in a negotiation. Although having clear goals and requirements is vital when negotiating (as I discuss earlier in 'Defining clear goals'), refusing to budge and getting bogged down in minutiae can cause you to lose sight of the overall goal and inadvertently kill the deal.

Negotiations fall apart every day because people get stuck on the finer points and fail to consider the larger framework. This problem often occurs when people with different communication preferences are negotiating. If you sense this is the case, identify the other person's preferred style and adjust yours accordingly. (For more about preferred styles, turn to Chapter 3.)

Keep the whole picture in mind so that you can control what may become a maze of issues as well as the number of concessions that you need to make (as I describe in the preceding section).

Respecting the relationship

You know your negotiation is successful when you and your counterpart meet your needs and preserve your relationship. In its fullest sense, negotiating develops long-term positive relationships and mutual respect for both sides.

Understanding other people's intentions and appreciating their needs and desires is the first step in building a respectful relationship. Trust is also essential for creating good relationships, and so make sure that you demonstrate the following attributes in order to construct respectful, trusting relationships:

- ✔ **Competence:** Good technical and interpersonal knowledge and skills.

- ✔ **Consistency:** Reliability, predictability and good judgement.

- ✔ **Integrity:** Honesty and truthfulness.

- ✔ **Loyalty:** Willingness to protect and save face for another person.

- ✔ **Openness:** Demonstrating honesty and truthfulness.

When you negotiate, demonstrate grace and style under pressure. Assess the person you're negotiating with and adjust your communication style as necessary. Listen, don't interrupt and avoid involving egos and emotions.

Determining the consequences

Throughout a negotiation, keep in mind the consequences for yourself and the other party. You want to make sure that everyone comes out feeling that they've succeeded and can hold their heads high.

If the people you're negotiating with end up feeling like losers, they may well lose enthusiasm for honouring the agreement and fulfilling the deal. People who sense that they've been treated unfairly are likely to find ways of wriggling out of the agreement. If they think that they're stuck with what's been agreed, the chances of them negotiating future deals with you are slim.

Knowing who holds the power

All negotiations are about power and it swings back and forth between individuals. By identifying the types of power that exist in the relationship, you can plan a strategy that can help you work successfully with the other party.

Some people shudder and flee when the word *power* is mentioned, whereas others grasp the idea with both hands as a means of coercing and forcing people to do their bidding. When I talk about 'power', however, I mean the ability to influence outcomes. Various types of power are capable of doing this during negotiations, depending on how you use them (see the sidebar 'Power positions' for some examples). Although power isn't inherently bad, its abuse is hideous.

One side in a negotiation seldom holds all the power. For example, if you go to a bank to ask for a loan, you hold power. 'What is she on?' I hear you say! Well, think about it: you decide which bank to approach, what to put up as collateral and whether or not you accept the bank's offer.

Power positions

In their research into social power in the 1950s, French and Raven identified different types of power, some of which I outline in the following list.

Although you may think that you have no power, everyone has power to some degree and exerts it in everyday life. For example, although you may have to answer to someone in higher authority than you, you may have information the other person needs. If you're in a position to hand out rewards and benefits, you can get others to act in a certain way. Be careful applying this type of power, because while it occasionally works well, its capacity is limited. For example, when someone has all the rewards they want, your powerful position is no longer effective. When you have knowledge and skills that others don't have, your power increases. The point is to recognise what kind of power you have and apply it diligently.

  Positional power: This type of power comes from a person's formal position in relation to another. Although marketing managers hold sway over the marketing department, they have little power as regards influencing human resources.

Information power: The person who holds the most knowledge or expertise wields tremendous power. How the individual uses the expertise and knowledge determines how much power he has.

Control of rewards and punishments: Those who can reward desired performance or punish offending behaviour hold power, such as managers who can allocate funds or the police who can hand out speeding tickets.

Alliances and networks: This is a combination of information and positional power.

Access to and control of agendas: The person or organisation who sets the agenda can control the ground rules in a negotiation. They can determine the introduction of items that are favourable to themselves and block those items that work against them.

Charisma or personal power: This is the type of power that comes from personal qualities or attributes that people admire or want for themselves.

When you start looking at power as a means of influence, you make better use of what you may not even realise you have.

Don't be surprised if you feel vulnerable about business negotiations. Dependence, vulnerability and power all impact on
relationships. Complex relationships, such as those in negotiations, are infused with a degree of dependency. Whether
you're the boss or the employee, you and the party you're
negotiating with need one another. You don't have to like
each other, but you do rely on one another for information,
co-operation and agreement.

This dependency can make you feel vulnerable because messing
up the relationship is risky. For example, your boss can sack
you or the person you're negotiating with may shut down the
discussion. But when you keep your intention clear and are
willing to listen to and understand what's important to the
other person, you can reduce your anxiety and stay focused
on achieving your goal.

Considering all solutions

No matter what you're negotiating, consider all the possible
options before deciding on one solution. When you rush to a
decision you may miss out on finding the best possible agreement. Focusing on and clarifying the interests you and the
other party share in common, as opposed to taking a position
and sticking rigidly to it, opens the gates to finding common
ground and arriving at a mutually satisfying outcome.

When your negotiation involves a long-standing or challenging
problem, suggest that everyone steps away from the formal
negotiation and holds a brainstorming session to create a list
of possible solutions. This approach can release energy and
unlock a solution that no one previously considered.

Summarising and clarifying as you go

Throughout the negotiation process make a point of summarising your understanding of what has been said. Doing so helps
to clarify points of agreement and highlight areas that have
been ignored, omitted or are still up for discussion.

Summarising and clarifying ensures that you and the other person are working for the same result and share a mutual understanding of the subject at hand. By taking the time to summarise as you go along, you can see where progress is being made and that a mutually satisfying conclusion can be reached.

Clarifying requires that you actively listen, which you can read about in Chapter 4.

Closing the Deal

After you've developed a relationship between yourself and the other people – with trust established on both sides – and both parties are in agreement, the time has come to close the deal. Asking questions such as 'What makes this solution particularly attractive to you?' and 'Do you agree that we should do it this way?', in addition to making your proposal and summarising your understanding, sets the stage for your final question, 'Then, we've reached agreement?' If the other party says 'Yes,' shake hands, make a public announcement or sign a contract. If they say, 'Not yet,' ask what concerns they still have. No matter how frustrated you may get, the philosophy behind successful negotiations is respect, understanding and mutuality. If people feel tricked or betrayed, they will walk away from you never to return.

Whatever you do, don't rush to get to the final proposition. If you push for an early commitment you may destroy trust and the other party may feel hijacked. Instead, contain your excitement about the proposal because emotions, whether positive or negative, can lead to mistakes, such as becoming too lenient or taking things for granted.

Formalising the idea that agreement has been reached by using a collaborative approach is more likely to yield long-term success than bullying, coercing or forcing people to agree before they're ready.

If, at the end of your negotiations, you're still not able to close the deal, be prepared to walk away. Rather than holding a grudge or getting into a cat fight with name-calling and threats, express your disappointment that although you've been unsuccessful in reaching an agreement this time, you look forward to continuing the relationship and future negotiations.

If you want to pick up more tips about negotiation, get hold of a copy of *Negotiating For Dummies* by Michael C. Donaldson (Wiley).

Chapter 11

Communicating Across Cultures

. . . .

In This Chapter

▶ Appreciating differences

▶ Understanding that context is vital

▶ Steering clear of problems

. . . .

*I*n today's 'globalised' world, international trade and tourist travel occur on a regular basis. As a result, understanding and respecting cultural differences, and being able to communicate effectively with people whose backgrounds, ethnicity and customs are different from yours, are vital for establishing and maintaining positive relationships and building business.

Knowledge is key to communicating successfully across borders. Appreciating differences, valuing diversity and avoiding stereotyping can help you steer clear of misunderstandings. Although religious, cultural and behavioural differences can be frustrating, when you demonstrate respect and practise patience, your ability to communicate across borders is hugely enhanced.

The subject of cultural differences is vast, fascinating and worthy of a book of its own. In this chapter I aim simply to whet your appetite by offering you a broad view of the different norms, values, beliefs and customs across the globe. In addition, I provide you with some tips for side-stepping potential cross-cultural mistakes and mishaps.

Respecting Cultural Differences

Although some people live and work in the same town all their lives and know the ins and outs of what's acceptable and what's not, many people today move from city to city and country to country as part of their ordinary lives. When career prospects or personal interests lead to you packing your bags and upping sticks, being aware that where you're going is bound to be different to where you come from gets you off on the right foot.

Cultural differences can cause communication problems, and so always act with patience and forgiveness. When you respond during a conversation, give people the benefit of the doubt and avoid jumping to conclusions.

I used to believe that I appreciated cultural differences and that people are essentially the same wherever you go. I was living in the middle of bustling Manhattan when I married my German husband, who'd grown up in a small village on the Baltic. Immediately following our wedding I moved to the quiet south Oxfordshire countryside of the UK, where my husband's business was located. Whereas I was used to falling to sleep to the sound of horns honking in New York, I now found myself drifting off to the bucolic hum of farmyard animals. I was married to a man from a culture different from mine and living in a country that was poles apart from what I was used to.

Everything in my life was turned upside down and I found myself floundering, confused and annoyed by what I was encountering. When I thought I was demonstrating interest, I was perceived as pushy, and what I thought was aloof behaviour was considered respectful. My father's only piece of advice at the time was, 'Take things slowly, aim to learn and don't judge. What seems odd to you is normal to them and what you think is natural, others perceive as peculiar.' True words and sage counsel.

Stereotyping and generalising

Often I hear people make comments like, 'Well, you know what the Russians/Germans/Asians are like,' 'She's American/French/British, which explains everything' or 'You can't trust anyone from that part of the world.' Such stereotyping is a sure way of setting up communication roadblocks.

Accepting cultural differences as normal and being interesting enough to want to learn about the values, beliefs and behaviours of people around the world allows you more easily to connect and communicate with individuals who are distinct and dissimilar from you.

Stereotyping and generalising aren't the same thing:

- **Stereotyping:** This is when you make an assumption based on basic and standard concepts. When you stereotype cultures, religions, nationalities or anyone whose belief system isn't the same as yours, you're heading into dangerous territory. For example, if you meet an Hispanic woman and assume that she has a large family because of her ethnic background, you're stereotyping her.

- **Generalising:** This is when you make a statement about common trends within a group, with the understanding that you need further information before you can apply your statement to the specific individual. Continuing the example from the preceding bullet, you're generalising if you say to yourself 'Hispanics tend to come from large families, I wonder if she does'.

Generalising is a starting point for getting to know someone, whereas stereotyping limits the possibilities of finding out more about someone and probably ends a relationship before it can begin.

Developing awareness of different cultures

Every culture has its own learned ways of acting, feeling, thinking and communicating. Although recent neuroscience studies indicate that the brains of people in different cultures vary and may influence how they think and conduct themselves within their own lands, culture continues to be an amalgamation of acquired beliefs, attitudes and behaviours passed on through the ages.

In some cultures, the individual reigns supreme. People in these *individualistic* cultures (for example, North America, the UK and Ireland, Scandinavia, Australia, the Netherlands and Belgium, France, Italy and India) are expected to look after themselves and their families and put the needs of others on the back burner, if they pay any attention to them at all. In other cultures, called *collectivistic,* individuals are more interconnected from birth (examples include Latin America, Indonesia, China, Japan, Pakistan, Thailand, South Korea, Spain and Arab countries). The strong, cohesive group is number one and can be counted on to provide protection in exchange for loyalty. These different cultures communicate according to their values and can be identified by the beliefs and behaviours shown in Table 11-1.

All cultures are dynamic and fluid and no culture is purely individualistic or purely collectivistic.

Table 11-1   Characteristics of Individualistic and Collectivistic Cultures

Individualistic Cultures	Collectivistic Cultures
The individual is autonomous and independent of groups	The individual is an interdependent part of groups
Individual and personal goals have priority	Group needs and goals have priority
Independence, leadership, achievement and self-fulfilment are valued	Group harmony, duty, obligation and security are valued
Behaviour is explained by individual attitudes and preferences	Behaviour is explained by group norms
Relationships are based on costs and benefits to the individual: if the costs exceed the advantages, a person curtails the relationship	Relationships are based on the needs of the group: if the relationship benefits the group but not an individual, the individual continues to stay in the relationship

In very simple terms:

✔ **Individualistic cultures** emphasise the priorities of the individual. Members are rewarded for behaving independently and working to achieve their personal goals. You hear people talk about 'me, my, I and mine'. Hiring and promotion practices are based on individual achievement and qualifications.

> ✔ **Collectivist cultures** value group identity in which members of the culture aim to fulfil the goals of the group. People speak in terms of 'we, us and our'. Family comes first and when applying for jobs and seeking career advancement, familial relations take precedence over expertise.

As regards communication, the two cultures mean that you may have to adapt your communication style in order to connect with your listeners. In addition to providing information, communication builds and maintains relationships with other people. According to social psychologists Yuri Miyamoto and Norbert Schwarz, individualistic cultures place a greater emphasis on providing information while the collectivists emphasise relationships. People from individualistic cultures like the US and France tend to be self-centred and focus on their individual goals. They speak directly to the point and prefer clarity in their conversations.

When speaking with people from individualistic cultures, be prepared to listen to them talk about their personal achievements, wealth and aspirations. When in conflict with individuals from individualistic cultures, be prepared for a dominating and competing conflict style, laced with aggressive and emotionally expressive language.

Collectivistic cultures tend to view their opposite as cold and unsupportive. Conversation in collectivistic cultures tends to focus on the group, harmony and loyalty. In China, for example, you would never disagree with other people's opinion in public in order to protect them from 'losing face' or damaging their reputations. The communication style tends to rely on avoidance, obliging and compromising. Avoid direct confrontations and saying 'no' to a request or an idea, because rejecting a suggestion in public destroys the group's harmony.

But cultural differences run deeper than a simple split into individualistic and collectivistic. When working in cultures different from your own you may find communication difficult due to different cultural beliefs, because people's patterns of thought – how they perceive and interpret the world – are based on their cultures. As a result, the same words can mean different things to people from different cultures, even when they speak the 'same' language, such as the English, Scottish, Welsh and Irish, and Americans, Australians and South

Africans. When the language is different, room for misinterpretation exists in translation.

Before doing business in cultures that differ from your own, have a look at the work of authors Fons Trompenaars, Charles Hampden-Turner, Edward T. Hall, Richard D. Lewis and Geert Hofstede. You can also develop your knowledge and intercultural skills by visiting www.argonautonline.com. I also suggest you pick up a copy of *Cross-Cultural Selling For Dummies* by Michael Soon Lee and Ralph R. Roberts (Wiley).

Appreciating norms, values and beliefs

Gender differences, accents and language barriers can make clear communication a challenge. When norms, values and beliefs (see the nearby sidebar 'What makes you, you') are also different, the challenge increases.

In cultures where the individual is supreme – mostly Western or individualistic cultures (check out the earlier section 'Developing awareness of different cultures') – assertiveness, expressiveness and competitiveness are valued. In Eastern and Southern cultures, however, harmony and co-operation are what's most important. Of course, you're going to find a fine mix of both of these concepts in all cultures, and so for now allow me to generalise, for, as I mention earlier in the 'Stereotyping and generalising' section, generalisations can open the door to understanding.

What makes you, 'you'

Norms are the guidelines that determine how individuals are expected to behave in specific situations. They define what's acceptable and appropriate behaviour in various and particular circumstances.

Values provide general guidelines for how to behave, and reflect what's most important and worthwhile to that culture.

Beliefs govern the way you think, the way you act and the way you speak. They're a result of your reaction to the norms and values of your culture and determine who you are.

Individualistic cultures tend to complete one task at a time. In these *monochronic* societies, multi-tasking is not the norm, because individuals distinguish between their business and their social lives, living by the rule that there's a time to work and a time to play.

People from other cultures (for example, the Middle East, Latin America and Africa) approach time differently. For them, flexibility is key. In these *polychronic* cultures, individuals can integrate their work and their social lives with no problem. Maintaining relationships and socialising matter more than completing tasks according to a fixed time-frame. In such cultures time is seen in an holistic manner, and so many events can take place at once.

If you're from an individualistic culture and are used to starting and finishing according to a planned agenda and working your way through a meeting point by point, be prepared to socialise for a long time before getting down to business in other cultures. Your colleagues from, say, Mexico, Saudi Arabia or other collectivist countries (see the earlier section 'Developing awareness of different cultures') offer you extended conversation over copious cups of coffee or tea as they spend time establishing social rapport to build trust and harmony. Check out Chapter 5 for more about rapport building.

Acknowledging customs and religious practices

When you believe that all cultures' customs and religious practices are equally worthy, and you're able to adapt your way of viewing and responding to people who are dissimilar from you, you're well on your way to communicating with clarity and being able to send and receive accurate and complete messages.

Whether you're Roman Catholic, Protestant, Jewish or Islamic, Sunni, Shiite or Sikh, Mormon, Hindu or Buddhist, or a member of any other religious organisation – or none – your beliefs are just as important and meaningful to you as other people's are to them. To quote the Dalai Lama: 'Every religion emphasises human improvement, love, respect for others, sharing other people's suffering. On these lines every religion has more or less the same viewpoint and the same goal.'

Treat others with the same consideration and respect with which you want to be treated. This doesn't mean, however, that you should treat others completely as you want to be treated, because what works for one person may not work for another. In other words, as George Bernard Shaw said, 'Do not do unto others as you would that they should do unto you. Their tastes may not be the same.'

Being flexible

Flexibility, adaptability and open-mindedness are the route to successful communication. In order to communicate effectively you need to acknowledge and appreciate the differences between yourself and others and strive to adapt your style to meet theirs. When you embrace and address differences, you're able to break barriers and produce clear lines of communication, mutual trust and creative thinking. The more flexible you are in the way you view the world, the more enlightened you can be.

Your cultural baggage is unique and probably different from many countries you visit or work in. Although the values, beliefs, concepts and behaviours of your host country may vary from yours, not all the individuals you meet may subscribe fully to their culture's habits and practices. Cultural differences are general guidelines to follow and you can always find individuals who don't fit your expectations.

The most frequently cited reason for assignment failure overseas is the employee's or family's inability to adjust, or their lack of the skills necessary to be successful in the host culture.

Following the locals

Just because you hear about the world becoming a 'global village', don't assume that all your behaviour and communication habits are acceptable in every country or city. Wherever you go, follow the leader. Observe the dress, body language, interaction and behaviour of people in the know to avoid communicating something you didn't intend or provoking misunderstandings. Miniskirts, bare midriffs and kissing in public may be acceptable in southern California, but in Dubai you can be sent to jail for such dress or behaviour.

Here are just a few more examples: when you're introduced to someone in China be punctual and bow instead of shaking hands; haggling is expected in the Mediterranean and the Middle East; smoking pot in Amsterdam is sometimes acceptable, but smoking even cigarettes in public in Singapore can land you a hefty fine.

If in doubt, ask those in the know and read up on protocol before boarding your flight.

Understanding Context

Context is vital when communicating across cultural borders. As a broad generalisation, the concepts of high and low context refer to how people from different cultures communicate:

- ✔ **High-context cultures:** High-context communicators tend to speak in an indirect and formal manner and rely on the message being understood through implication. Examples of high-context cultures are most countries in Asia, the Middle East, Africa and South America.

- ✔ **Low-context cultures:** Here, the actual spoken words convey the intended meaning. People from low-context cultures are direct and informal in style and rely on the literal and precise meaning of the words they use, preferring explicit conversations. Low-context cultures include the UK and US, Germany, Switzerland, Israel and the Scandinavian countries.

Table 11-2 offers a brief outline of what to look for in high- and low-context cultures.

Table 11-2	Attributes of High- and Low-Context Cultures
High Context	*Low Context*
Indirect, formal and implied messages	Direct, informal and clear messages
Polychronic (fluid sense of time; multi-tasking)	Monochronic (segmented sense of time; tasks done one at a time)
High use of non-verbal communication	Little use of non-verbal communication
Little reliance on written communication	High reliance on written communication
Decisions based on intuition and feelings	Decisions based on facts and evidence
Long-term relationships	Short-term relationships
Relationships take precedence over schedules	Schedules take precedence over relationships

Spelling things out: Low-context cultures

When interacting with direct communicators from low-context cultures, expect to be told it like it is because they tend to say exactly what they mean. They're explicit in style and believe that saying what you have to say is better than letting people guess what you mean. They value logic, facts and directness and base their decisions on fact rather than intuition. Such people ask for explanations when they're unclear about the message and their communication is linear, with a steady stream of words.

According to cultural researchers William Gudykunst and Ting-Toomey, when speaking with people from low-context cultures, you can expect conversation to be direct, straight-forward, concise and efficient in relaying what actions people are to take at the end of a discussion. In their pursuit of clarity, they use precise words and expect them to be taken literally.

Space and culture

During his service in the US Army in Europe and the Philippines during World War II, the American anthropologist Edward T. Hall observed the difficulties that result from the basic differences within intercultural communication. He developed his theory of *proxemics,* or the study of the way humans use space within different cultures. In his book *The Hidden Dimension* (1966), he analysed the personal spaces that people form around their bodies.

His theory suggests that people maintain different degrees of personal distance according to the social setting and their cultural backgrounds. For example, people in the US for the most part engage in conversation at a distance of roughly 10–18 centimetres, whereas in many parts of continental Europe the distance is half that amount. This difference in space can lead to visiting Americans travelling overseas frequently feeling the need to back away from someone who's speaking with them because their territory is being invaded.

Inferring, suggesting and implying: High-context cultures

People who receive and deliver information through suggestion, implication and inference believe that not everything needs to be spoken out loud. Their communication style is influenced by the closeness of their relationships, the well-defined structure of their society and clear ways of behaving. Because they know what they mean without being explicit, they expect that listeners understand what they're saying.

When interacting with people from high-context cultures, sharpen your listening and observational skills (I discuss active listening in Chapter 4). To understand the message fully you have to read between the lines and interpret nonverbal signals.

Watching your body language abroad

Body language can mean different things in different cultures. What's perfectly acceptable in one country is considered rude and shocking in another. Here's a brief list of actions that mean different things to different people:

- **Eye contact.** In most individualistic, low-context countries, intermittent eye contact is important for conveying interest and attention. In many Middle Eastern countries intense eye contact between the same genders demonstrates trust and sincerity. But anything other than the briefest eye contact between opposite genders is considered inappropriate. Extended eye contact in African, Asian and Latin American cultures is considered a challenge, and the Japanese are uncomfortable with even the briefest eye contact.

- **Facial expressions.** According to American psychologist Paul Ekman, there is a basic set of six universal facial expressions that carry the same meaning across the world. These expressions are happiness, sadness, fear, anger, disgust and surprise. In many Mediterranean cultures, people exaggerate signs of sadness and it's not uncommon for both men and women to cry in public. Japanese and Chinese men, however, would rather not reveal their anger, sorrow, confusion or disgust in public for fear of losing face. In Japan, a smile can also mask an emotion or be used to avoid answering a question. The Japanese may also smile when they're embarrassed and laugh to conceal their anger.

- **Gestures.** Gestures are frequently used to replace the spoken word and are specific to a given culture. While one gesture, such as the 'Oh' sign – in which the thumb and index finger form a circle – means 'OK' in English-speaking countries and amongst the scuba-diving population, the French interpret the sign as 'worthless', the Japanese read it as 'money' and the Greeks interpret the gesture as a sexual insult. In Western cultures the 'Thumbs-Up' gesture indicates a job well done, while in the Middle East, Latin America, Africa, Greece, Russia and southern Italy, the gesture equates to a raised middle finger.

- **Spatial awareness.** Perceptions of space are moulded and patterned by culture. People from Latin countries, for example, are most comfortable when they're up close and personal, while North Americans need more space when engaging in conversation. In England, queuing is a natural way of life, whereas in China and Korea, pushing to get to the front is typical. When driving, the English tend to adhere to traffic laws, while in most Middle Eastern, African and Asian countries, beeping horns and cutting others up is a normal part of the highway code.

When speaking to people who can infer what you're saying, you can expect to speak without being interrupted. People from high-context cultures tend to rely on verbal and non-verbal cues for understanding the speaker's meaning and talk around the point rather than addressing it directly. Intuition and feelings take precedence over logic and reason. Tone of voice, facial expressions, gestures and posture hold more weight than words. When communicating with each other, their language is indirect, ambiguous, harmonious, reserved and understated. As a Japanese colleague said to me, 'We are a homogeneous people and don't have to speak as much as you do. When we say one word, we understand ten, whereas you have to say ten to understand one.'

People from high-context cultures focus on the group, rather than the individual, and so they strive to maintain harmony in their interactions, relying on implication to convey their messages. When they're confronted with conflict, they do whatever they can to avoid dealing with it directly. In order to 'save face' – or maintain another person's reputation and the respect of other people – avoid engaging in direct conflict with someone from a high-context culture.

Avoiding the Pitfalls

The differences between individualistic, low-context cultures (in which direct communication and a bit of dramatic flair are the norm) and collectivistic, high-context cultures (in which implication, inference and subtlety are paramount) mean that intercultural communication is fraught with potential pitfalls.

Here are a few tips to bear in mind:

- Steer clear of inappropriate humour; if in doubt, hold your tongue.
- Stop, listen and reflect before speaking, to ensure that you take your surroundings and context into account.
- Consider your vocal quality and body language when you communicate.

To help you avoid making major communication gaffs, have a look at Table 11-3. Based on the Richard Lewis Communications Ltd model (www.crossculture.com) it helps to clarify what values each culture holds sacred and its preferred way of communicating.

Table 11-3   Values and Communication Styles of the Different Culture Types

Individualistic, Low-Context Cultures	Collectivistic, High-Context Cultures
Values	**Values**
Democracy	Hierarchies
Self-determinism	Fatalism
Female equality	Male dominance
Work ethic	Work ethic
Human rights	Inequality
Ecology	Exploits environment
Communication Style	**Communication Style**
Extrovert	Introvert
Forceful	Modest
Lively	Quiet
Thinks aloud	Thinks in silence
Interrupts	Doesn't interrupt
Talkative	Dislikes big talkers
Uncomfortable with silence	Uses silence
Truth before diplomacy	Diplomacy before truth
Overt body language	Little body language

© Richard D. Lewis

Part V
Communicating Across Distances

'It's all very well communicating in
an old-fashioned way, but there is always
the danger of being overheard.'

In this part...

*I*n these chapters I let you in on the power of modern-day technology and old-fashioned practices to communicate your messages in ways that engage other people and make them want to connect with you. You pick up tips for making an outstanding impression, getting your point across and raising your profile so that when you call, write, text or email, people want to hear from you.

Chapter 12

Communicating Successfully through Technology

Communicating through electronic technology is a normal part of everyday life. Emailing, texting and Skyping as well as tweeting, blogging and connecting through webinars are just some of the ways people keep in touch.

But as the choice of communication methods rises, the danger of making mistakes increases. In this chapter I offer you a few pointers for ensuring that your technological communications are clear and appropriate no matter what form of social media or online interaction you're using. I show you how to appear professional when necessary, observe the protocols and adhere to the correct etiquette.

Getting Your Email Etiquette Right

Although many people may struggle to recall a world before electronic mail (email), the form is a relative newcomer to the communication community, becoming a regular part of every-day life only since the mid-1990s. Of course from time to time you still prefer to send a letter through the mail (so-called snail mail), but email is perfect for:

✔ Immediate requests for information

✔ Quick congratulations or good news messages

✔ Speedy responses

A common problem with many emails, however, is senders addressing multiple topics in a single email. Readers then become confused as to what they're meant to do, deleting or filing the emails away with no further action.

To prevent this fate happening to your emails, write a separate one for each subject you want to address so that:

✔ The email is easy to read and understand.

✔ The recipient knows what you expect and can take appropriate action based on your request.

✔ The recipient can file the email in the folder reserved for information on that topic.

When you write separate emails for different subjects, you receive clearer answers.

Email is a quick and effective way of communicating but can be a distraction at work. Put into place the following guidelines to make best use of company time and resources:

✔ Avoid replying to every email the moment it arrives. Instead, set up designated times for checking your inbox and responding.

✔ Shut down your email software when you have an important task to complete.

✔ Acknowledge receipt of long or complex emails that require time and attention in order to give a proper response; let the sender know that you plan to reply as soon as possible.

✔ Establish and enforce an email policy. Draft this policy with the help of Human Resources, IT and the company's Board of Directors in order to reflect all viewpoints in the organisation. Write the policy in clear and simple language, and do not exceed four pages. Update the policy at least once a quarter and enforce it through an acceptable use policy (AUP) and electronic monitoring. Knowing that messages are reviewed and stored is one way of curtailing improper use of the system. Here are some points to include in your policy:

- Commercial guidelines, such as style, signatures, timing for responding to emails, who to cc: or bcc:, what to do when you receive emails and guidelines on forwarding emails.

- Rules on using the email system, including compliance, creating a safe working environment, preventing leakage of confidential information and preventing the abuse of the system, such as circulating non-essential attachments like family photos or holiday videos.

- Legal considerations, including associated risks.

✔ When replying to an email, stick to the same subject and put your response at the top. Don't make the receiver dig through all the text to get to your point.

✔ Retain the content of emails that you receive. Unless they contain something inappropriate or unnecessary for your recipient to see, maintain transparency in all communications.

✔ Respect people's time. Only send email messages that are necessary and relevant.

Email secrets

Sky Broadband reveals that 51 per cent of British workers prefer to send emails than use the phone to speak to colleagues, 25 per cent don't want their boss to see the emails they've been sending at work and 11 per cent have flirted with someone they shouldn't have through email. What a tangled web we weave!

Poor emails cost jobs!

Donna's job as a marketing manager involved introducing new clients to the firm and maintaining positive relationships with existing customers. Yet during a whole year of work she failed to acquire one new client and several existing customers resisted renewing their contracts. Her boss, Nancy, received complaints about Donna's long, often overly familiar emails, which Nancy knew nothing about because Donna failed to copy her in. The emails were frequently six or more single-spaced paragraphs long, poorly written with many grammatical and spelling errors, and contained information the client didn't need to know. Donna overloaded her emails and didn't take into account the readers' needs, communication style, personal preferences or limited time. As a result, she alienated existing clients and put off potential ones. Nancy had to scramble to get her business back on track and Donna lost her job.

Appearing your best in emails

When sending an email, make sure that your writing skills present you well and enable your reader to decipher what you're saying quickly and accurately. For example:

- ✔ Limit yourself to three paragraphs for congratulations, good news or a request:

  - First paragraph contains the news or request.

  - Second paragraph contains the details.

  - Final paragraph is a courteous closing.

- ✔ Use appropriate sentence structure, grammar and punctuation. Avoid Internet acronyms such as 'LOL' (laugh out loud) if you're writing in a professional capacity. If you're writing to a friend, or someone you write to on a frequent basis, of course be more informal.

- ✔ Set up a signature at the bottom of your email that includes your full name, position, company name, phone numbers and email address. Doing so saves you time and gives the appropriate information to each person you communicate with.

✔ Avoid sending an inappropriate email that's written in haste or anger. Make sure that you write only what you're comfortable with anyone reading.

Thinking of your reader

Whenever you send emails, think of the readers: what do they need to know and how do they like to take in information? Always treat them with respect. Also, time is money, so keep your messages short and succinct. Many people receive 50 or more emails a day, so don't try to 'wow' them with purple prose. The point of an email is to convey information simply, quickly and clearly. Flip to Chapter 3 for loads more about communication styles and preferences, and read the nearby sidebar 'Poor emails cost jobs!' for how not to email.

Never send an email – solicited or not – without first doing your research. If you ask questions that can be found easily on the company's website you're unwittingly indicating that you're lazy, a bit dull, dim and slow on the uptake. In addition, don't send an email to a random recipient with an opening along the lines of, 'I'm not sure if you're the right person for me to write to, but I guess you'll pass this message on.' Don't guess! People are busy and if you can't be bothered to write to the right person, you can't expect the recipient to bother responding or forwarding your message.

Do your research and say why you're writing to the particular individual. An opening line such as, 'I am writing to you because I understand that you are the person responsible for. . .' shows that you've done your homework and are familiar with the organisation.

Creating a distinctive and descriptive subject line

With the amount of emails winging their way into people's in-boxes, you want to make yours stand out from the crowd by being clear and meaningful.

Think of your subject lines as newspaper headlines (without the groan-inducing puns). They're intended to capture your readers' attention and draw them into the content, so ensure that your subject line clearly identifies the content in your email message. For example, a clear and succinct subject line like 'Application for marketing position listing 8686KlK' or 'Agenda items for 17 April meeting listed below' alerts your readers to the content of the message and prepares them for what's to follow.

Readers are likely to delay opening your email (if they open it at all) if the subject line is weak. And if the subject line is blank, you're giving recipients a good reason for ignoring your email or hitting the delete button.

Subject lines such as 'read this', 'important information' and 'for your consideration' are meaningless. All emails you send are meant to be read and contain information worthy of your recipients' attention. If your emails don't pass this criterion, don't bother sending them. For information about subject lines for marketing campaigns, pick up a copy of *E-Mail Marketing For Dummies* by John Arnold (Wiley).

Registering a professional-sounding address

Email is an integral part of today's social and professional life, so your email address needs to show you in your best light. Think of it like a calling card that you'd hand out to prospective clients and other businesses. Although a clever or fun email name may amuse your friends and family, a prospective client or employer is likely to wonder about your suitability if your name sounds unprofessional. I once received an email responding to a job offer from cuteguy@fakemail.com. He didn't get an interview.

Being self-employed and working from home, like many people do, doesn't mean that you shouldn't be respected in the business world. If you choose an email address that includes your local cable or phone company as your host, you're sending out a message that you're small fry in the world of commerce. Opt instead for a web-hosting company that can offer relatively inexpensive packages, including email accounts for your domain name that make you look like a bigger player than you may be.

Start your search by going to www.10bestwebhosting.co.uk.

The dangers of getting fancy

Many people have problems using HTML (Hyper-text Markup Language) formatted email. Although such emails are more attractive than plain text, with embedded images and objects and the ability to create interactive forms, if your recipient's computer isn't configured correctly to interpret the email, it may be impossible to open or view. Also, anti-spam filters can intercept such emails and block some of the content or cause them to be undeliverable.

An option that allows for several different basic email accounts such as `info@yourcompany.com` or `sales@yourcompany.com` offers you some level of anonymity and allows for expansion or change in personnel without changing an account name. In addition, having several names again implies that your company is a significant player.

If you don't have a website, set up an email account with a web-based provider such as Yahoo! or Gmail and establish an address that reflects your job or experience. For example, if you're a home-based interior decorator, create an address like `Decorate4You@yahoo.com` or `YourDecorator@gmail.com`.

When you choose a name, consider how it represents you; it influences how email receivers perceive and respond to you.

Numbers are perfectly acceptable and professional for email addresses as are combinations of numbers and initials. This is a particularly effective form for protecting your identity. For example, because teachers are sometimes targets of unpleasant emails from angry students and resentful parents, they commonly choose their initials and their birth date – or another favourite number – as their email address to protect their identity. For example, `elk8686@school.com` would be acceptable although `playboy4you@institution.com` may raise some eyebrows.

Keeping your formatting simple

When you send an email, keep in mind that the people receiving your message have different computer systems, networks and email browser configurations impacting on how they see your message. What looks one way on your computer may come across differently on someone else's.

Email marketing campaigns, including newsletters and email promotions, are a vital part of business today and the format you use can make your message look top-notch or a mess. I focus here on formatting for basic email correspondence, which is a simple way of keeping a written record of what you communicate.

One of the benefits of sending an email in *plain text* (in which only the words are transmitted) is that it's easy to compose, send and receive. In addition, plain-text emails never contain viruses or cause security problems. Great news for anyone receiving an email from you! On the other hand, plain text doesn't allow for pictures, graphics, colours or different sized letters or types of font and so your emails can look quite dull. For problems on using other formats, check out the nearby sidebar 'The dangers of getting fancy'.

To reflect a professional profile in your emails, stick to a simple format, similar to what you find in a business letter: be short, clear and concise. (For more about writing letters, turn to Chapter 14.) Follow the suggestions below to deliver a message that's sure to be read:

✔ Limit your emails to one printed page when possible.

✔ Stick to one paragraph per point and double space between paragraphs.

✔ Bullet your points to express your thoughts clearly.

✔ Write your emails in upper- and lower-case letters to make them easy to read.

If you send emails in plain text be aware that the message can be intercepted and read. Although the risk is small, use encryption to scramble sensitive data before sending and never ask customers to send the sensitive data in emails.

Watching for danger points

You face a number of management, security and privacy issues when using email in your business. Because email is a common source of computer virus infections, adhere to the following precautions to protect yourself and others:

✔ Employ an anti-virus device to scan all incoming and out-going emails for security threats.

✔ Be cautious of emails containing unexpected attachments and never open suspect ones.

A disclaimer in an email reminds anyone receiving the message – especially those dealing with privileged or confidential information – that they aren't to disclose the content of the email under any circumstances. If the information is revealed, however, you can do little about it, unless the individual who let the cat out of the bag is a licensed professional. In such a case, even if the disclosure happened inadvertently, the action may constitute professional malpractice.

As much as I'd like to say that email disclaimers and confidentiality notices act as binding contracts, lawyers suggest that they don't. The Internet is an open network that allows anyone to connect with anyone else, making global communication a breeze on the one hand and causing countless security concerns on the other. Because emails are there for all to see – if you care enough and have the patience to track them down – they are automatically part of the public record. That being said, individuals in the legal profession do advise clients to use disclaimers, because a solicitor tells me 'they trigger provisions of the Code of Professional Responsibility with respect to the unintentional release of confidential information.' Spoken like a true solicitor!

A disclaimer isn't a legal and binding contract: it's a way for the sender to remind individuals of their obligation to keep the information to themselves.

Making the Most of Social Media

The purpose of *social media* is to create interactive communication between individuals, communities and organisations. The technology has many different electronic forms including Internet forums, blogs and podcasts. Because of the vast and ever-increasing amount of social media available and the excellent coverage of the topic in *Social Media Marketing For Dummies* by Shiv Singh and *Social Media Metrics For Dummies* by Leslie Poston (both Wiley), I offer just a few brief thoughts on how to make the most of the best-known social media forms: Facebook, Twitter and LinkedIn.

Representing yourself on Facebook

Facebook is a great way of promoting yourself, whether you're letting friends and family know about your amazing life or you want to gain an edge on your business competition by creating a powerful presence.

Nurture and build the relationship with everyone you befriend on Facebook. For business purposes, the more Facebook friends you have, the more people discover who you are and how you can serve their organisations.

Here are some suggestions for developing rapport on Facebook built on trust:

- **Post regularly:** Add to your page every day but don't go overboard. Too many posts create the impression that you have nothing else to do, and you may lose friends who can block or hide your updates. To make yourself visible, 2–3 posts per day is about right.

- **Include personal data:** Although business content is interesting, adding personal information helps people get to know you better. By understanding what appeals and is important to you, people become more engaged with you and develop confidence in what you can offer.

  When providing personal information, be circumspect in what you write. A potential boss won't find your drunken night of reverie as amusing as you do.

- **Keep it short:** Stick to a maximum of 100 words. Any longer and people lose interest.

- **Ask for interaction:** Some ideas include:

    • Reach out to your friends for help, whether you have a problem to solve or need something clarifying. People like to connect and become involved. When they do, they also get public credit on your page.

- Post a funny picture or cartoon and ask people to come up with a caption. Not only do you get some amusing answers, but also people look forward to the next one. Make this a weekly or monthly habit.

- Invite people to share some personal details. Perhaps create a short list of likes and dislikes they can share. You can also include something business related, such as 'I feel the most important Search Engine Optimisation feature on my website is. . .'. By engaging others you build their interest in you.

- Ask people about their own businesses and request links that they find useful. Even if they don't have businesses, they're sure to have some bits of information they can share and you never know what gems they may come up with. Sharing information is a great way of keeping people coming back to your page.

✔ **Follow up:** When people interact with you on your Facebook page, make sure that you thank them for their input. When you share comments about their participation they're likely to return to the page where they get public recognition.

✔ **Include links:** When you provide links to your blog or your website, you improve your Facebook presence. In addition, link from other social media and websites because the more links you have on your page, the more connected you are.

If you want to get the full lowdown on Facebook, pick up a copy of *Facebook For Dummies* by Carolyn Abram (Wiley).

Twittering and tweeting

Twitter is one of the most popular social networking tools, used by celebrities, politicians and business organisations as well as the likes of you and me. It's a 'place' where you can share information as it happens, connecting with others in real time. Twitter can add to your life by boosting your business and keeping up with friends and individuals and organisations you're interested in knowing more about.

Twitter offers you the opportunity to share your thoughts and activities with the rest of the world, or at least those who care enough to sign up to your account, in short steady bursts. By

posting entries (called *tweets*) of no more than 140 characters, including spaces, you can communicate with friends and
family as well as celebs and political and business leaders.

Using Twitter is fairly simple when you get used to the terminology and technology. The best place to find out how to use
and enjoy Twitter is *Twitter For Dummies* by Michael Gruen
and Leslie Poston (Wiley). Here you discover how to get set
up, build a list of followers and find your own voice for tweeting through the ether.

Some of the rules and etiquette for Twitter include:

- ✔ **Be selective:** Following a load of people and only being
  followed by a few sends a message that you're ready to
  spam. Sending out constant tweets encouraging people
  to sign up for your blog or RSS feed indicates that you're
  a spammer. This is no way to build up a list of followers
  who are really interested in what you have to say.

- ✔ **Credit retweets:** Sharing interesting tweets makes you
  look generous and interested in what others have to say.
  The format looks like: 'Retweet @ psb: Interactive broad-
  cast with special guest! http://tinyurl.com/psb.
  Not to be missed!'

- ✔ **Follow your followers:** When you first join, this is a great
  way of building up followers. As your list grows, weed
  out the ones whose conversations don't interest you.

- ✔ **No more than 140 characters:** That's all you get, so keep
  your message clear and creative. Think: short, sharp,
  snappy!

- ✔ **Stick to the style:** Write in real words rather than using
  abbreviations unless you're really strapped for space.

Getting LinkedIn

Businesspeople have discovered the benefits of belonging to
LinkedIn, a business-only social network that currently has
over 48 million members in more than 200 countries. LinkedIn
is like a sophisticated online business card where you create
a profile that showcases your skills and attracts contacts. You
can find and connect with former associates and new acquaintances as well as search for a job, develop sales leads and
market your services.

Like all social networking sites LinkedIn has its own form of rules and etiquette, right and wrong ways of promoting yourself and your business. *LinkedIn For Dummies* by Joel Elad (Wiley) gives you a great in-depth picture of how to use LinkedIn to best effect, but for now check out the following tips as a jumping-off place:

- ✔ **Know the people you want to connect with or get someone you both know to introduce you.** If you try to connect with people you don't know they can push the 'I don't know' button. Five 'I don't know' hits and your ability to invite others to connect is limited.

- ✔ **Proofread your posts.** Misspelling the name of your school and university or previous employers makes you look incompetent. LinkedIn is where you can build your professional profile, so don't be sloppy.

- ✔ **Add a professional photograph of yourself.** Remember that LinkedIn is a site for career building, not getting a date. Save the photos of you looking hot at the beach for Facebook (see the earlier 'Representing yourself on Facebook' section).

- ✔ **Keep your profile up to date and complete.** Get all your relevant professional information listed in your complete profile and check your account daily so that you can stay current with what's happening in the business community and with your contacts.

Employing Other Forms of Electronic Communication

Every day seems to offer novel ways of communicating over the Internet with clients, colleagues, friends and family members. As communication over the airways becomes the norm, new protocols and challenges present themselves. The section below addresses some of these to help you communicate with finesse.

Working your way around the web

Through the web of technological mechanisms, people around the world and well into space can see and speak with one another, passing on information and gaining knowledge. Here are some of the available options:

- ✔ **Webcast:** A one-way means of communicating to a large audience. President Obama makes use of webcasts when his speeches are presented live.

- ✔ **Webinar:** Allows you to present information and attendees to interact with you. For example, you can poll live attendees in real time, push out real-time results to the attendees and discuss the findings. You can also include a live Q&A session.

- ✔ **Web meetings:** Mostly helpful for formal presentations to small groups. They can even be one-to-one, such as for a coaching situation when you and your coach can't meet face to face. One example, WebEx, allows you to join via a login link and a dial-in connection. Web meetings can be fully interactive, with the leader sharing their screen, providing demonstrations and walking people through the information. Less formal than webcasts and webinars, web meetings are expected to be fully interactive because the point is to generate dialogue and collaboration among attendees.

For more detailed information about communicating through the web, grab yourself a copy of *WebEx Web Meetings For Dummies* by Nancy Stevenson (Wiley).

Keeping in touch with texts

Texting is a way of sending and receiving a short message (160 characters or less, including spaces) from one mobile phone to another. Also known as SMS (Short Message Service), texting is a great way of communicating, especially when making a phone call is out of the question.

Wherever you look these days, fingers are flying on the small keyboards of mobile phones, sending messages to friends, family, clients and colleagues all over the world. Because of the zest for real-time communication, you may forget your manners as your need to communicate overtakes your respect for others. Therefore, bear in mind the following basic ground rules for texting:

- ✔ **Don't text for the sake of texting.** Don't send messages unless you have something important to say.

- ✔ **Reply as soon as you can.** If you get a message that asks, 'Will u b @ the pub 2nite?' put your manners into practice and reply with a 'y' for yes or an 'n' for no.

✔ **Never propose or break up a relationship via text.** Some messages are meant to be communicated face-to-face, no matter how challenging.

✔ **Be selective where and when you text.** Refrain from texting when you're on a date, at a party, in a group, at work or at the movies, theatre or a concert. Unless an emergency arises, put your phone away and stay focused on your job and the people you're with.

✔ **Make sure that you follow up with a phone call or go to the person directly if you must apologise through a text message.** You can then start by asking if the other person received your text.

✔ **Never answer stray messages.** Also, don't give out personal information via a text message.

✔ **Watch your texting lingo.** By all means send acronyms to your close friends, but use 'real' words when communicating with a client or your boss.

✔ **Stick to the well-established shorthand texting codes.** Making codes up as you go along means that others have to stop and think about what you're trying to say.

✔ **Don't forward personal texts to other people.** Forwarding a personal text is akin to gossiping.

✔ **Consider the feelings and comfort of the people you're with.** Keeping your nose stuck to your keypad when you're with others is rude and insulting. When you're with real people in real time, shut your phone off and enjoy the present moment.

Finding your voice through VoIP

Until recently, the most common communication system in the world (apart from talking!) was the standard analogue telephone service. But now VoIP (Voice over Internet Protocol), which uses digital data to allow you to see the people you're speaking with as well as hearing them, lets you communicate with your next-door neighbour or a stranger on the other side of the globe at little or no charge, depending on the service you choose. VoIP calls are an easy and accessible way to keep in touch with family and friends.

You can choose from loads of VoIP options. The best known is Skype, but others include Voxox, Goober Messenger, Viber,

Google Hangouts, Tiny chat and VBuzzer among many others. To get started, all you need are an online computer, a web-camera, speakers and a headset with a microphone. You can even call from mobile phones and if you really want to stay connected, call while you're travelling, sitting on the beach or in the bath!

As with any new technology, VoIP has advantages (low costs, flexibility and increased productivity due to the emerging applications) and drawbacks. The latter include:

- ✔ **Connection down:** VoIP depends on your broadband connection. When your connection goes down, so does your phone line, which is annoying for home use but potentially catastrophic for business.

- ✔ **Echo:** You can hear your own voice after a few milliseconds. Although you may also hear an echo on your standard phone system, the echo on a VoIP is more annoying because it normally has more delay.

- ✔ **Emergency calls:** Regulators don't require VoIP providers to offer emergency calls, like 999 or 911, and so some don't. This isn't such a problem because when you're making an emergency call you go for the quickest form of communication, which would be your landline, mobile or shouting out at the top of your lungs.

- ✔ **Shared connection:** If you're using a broadband connection for your data and communication needs – downloads, connectivity, chat, email and so on – peak times of usage can leave you with inadequate bandwidth.

- ✔ **Voice quality:** You hear the sound later than you should, breaking the flow of the conversation. When the delay is constant and not too long, however, your conversation can be acceptable.

  The sound delay isn't always constant and varies depending on technical factors. This variation in delay is called *jitter,* which damages the voice quality.

- ✔ **Security:** Identity and service theft, viruses, call tampering, spamming and phishing attacks are prominent security issues with VoIP.

If you're interested in finding out more about VoIP, get a copy of *VoIP For Dummies* by Timothy V. Kelly or *Skype For Dummies* by Loren Abdulezer, Susan Abdulezer and Howard Dammond (both from Wiley).

Chapter 13

Communicating over the Phone

I wonder whether you're thinking, 'I don't need this chapter. . . I know how to talk on the telephone!' Well, perhaps, but a big difference exists between chatting casually on the phone and communicating effectively and successfully, especially in a business context.

You're always creating an impression of some sort. Whenever you make a phone call – for business or personal reasons – how you speak and sound to other people determines how they perceive you, and if it's a business call, how they perceive the organisation you work for.

Although I focus in this chapter on business calls, many of the principles apply equally to personal calls.

Calling with Confidence

I'm always astonished when someone calls me and then sounds surprised when I pick up the phone. Even when I let the call go to voice mail, the speaker at the other end often sounds unprepared and unsure as to the reason for the call.

I've heard all forms of stuttering, speed-speaking, um-ing and ah-ing while I struggle to understand who the caller is and what they want.

When you call someone, save time and effort for both of you by knowing the purpose of your call. Take charge from the start; after all, you're the one calling.

In this section I offer you some simple tips for sounding in charge.

Preparing in advance

Just because you pick up the phone and dial a number doesn't mean that you want to speak to the person you're calling. Although that statement may seem counterintuitive, consider occasions when you're calling on someone else's behalf or delivering bad news. Even if you do want to speak to the person you're calling, being prepared is fundamental, especially when the call relates to business. Because time is precious in today's fast-paced world, most people don't have enough hours in their day or patience to listen to you um and ah at the other end of the line while you gather your thoughts.

To get you through phone calls with as little pain as possible, jot down an outline of what you want to say and keep it close by while you speak. Tick off the points as you make them to be sure that you cover everything you want to say.

If you want to make an appointment, have some convenient times in mind. If your call goes to voice mail, repeat your name and number twice, speaking slowly and distinctly. You can also leave an email address as an alternative to a phone number. As I say in Chapter 3, different people have different preferences for communicating.

Managing the opening efficiently

Always identify yourself when making a business phone call. Leaping into the conversation, saying 'Guess who?' or 'It's me' is annoying, unprofessional and sounds silly. State your full name and the company you're calling from. If the call goes to voice mail, add your phone number so that the receiver can return your call.

Having identified yourself, state the purpose of your call. For example, you can say, 'Hello. This is [name] from [your company]. I'm calling [name of person you're calling] to speak with him/her about [purpose].' You can make yourself sound extra polite by asking, 'Is now a convenient time to speak?' This is especially important when you call someone on their mobile phone as they could be in an awkward situation.

Never start with 'Who am I speaking with?' Identify yourself first and then ask 'To whom am I speaking?'

Getting to your point

Time is money and although you want to be polite, you don't need to get involved in long, personal conversations. When you know the people you're calling, of course you may ask how they are, but then get to the point of your call. Becoming involved in a lengthy personal conversation or office gossip is inappropriate and a waste of your time and theirs.

If your call goes to voice mail, keep your message short and succinct. Making someone listen to long, unnecessary chit-chat before getting to the point is annoying and makes you sound like you don't know why you called. (Check the earlier 'Preparing in advance' section to ensure that you *do* know!)

Speaking clearly

If you're going to speak, speak clearly. Enunciate, talk directly into the mouth piece and avoid mumbling. Speak loudly enough to be heard by the person you're calling and not so loudly that everyone within earshot is privy to your private conversation.

Always remain aware of people around you and speak discreetly, especially when you're in public places. Remember, the person sitting next to you may overhear confidential information that, if it becomes public, may negatively affect your business.

In Chapter 7, I offer you lots of ways to make your voice clear and resonate.

Asking for what you want

Instead of beating around the bush and spending time on small talk, let the person you're calling know the reason upfront and ask for what you want. Don't keep people guessing.

I recently received a phone call from a colleague. She asked if I could give her 5–10 minutes of my time to speak with her about an issue she was facing at work. Because she was clear about what she wanted and our relationship is based on respect and trust, I felt confident that she'd stick to the time frame and get to the point.

Check out Chapter 2 for more about communicating your message clearly.

Dealing Professionally with Received Calls

How you receive a call reflects the organisation you work for as well as your personal style. Because you may be the first and only contact the caller has with your company, aim to make a good impression. For simple techniques for creating a positive impact, follow the tips I provide in this section.

Picking up promptly

Aim to answer your call within three rings. Any more than that and your caller may think that no one's there and hang up.

When you do pick up, be sure that you're not engaged in another conversation, drinking, eating or chewing gum. The phone amplifies noise and the sounds of whispering, slurping and smacking lips create a really bad impression.

If you're away from your desk for more than a few minutes, divert your calls to voice mail to make sure that no calls go unanswered.

Greeting callers cheerfully

When you pick up the phone, always identify yourself and the name of the organisation; doing so confirms to callers that they have the right number. Speaking clearly and distinctly creates a good first impression.

My PA, Charlotte, has a cheery, upbeat tone to her voice. Clients frequently tell me that when she answers the phone saying, 'Kuhnke Communication. Charlotte speaking,' they end up smiling and feeling cheerful.

When you speak in a pleasant tone of voice you have a positive effect on your caller's attitude. Read Chapter 6 for more about the power of positive attitude.

Offering to help

Always ask how you can help callers. Doing so makes them feel that you care about them and helps to keep people focused. If they go off on an unrelated riff, not getting to the point of the call, asking what you can do to help gets them back on track.

Sometimes callers reach the wrong number or department. When that happens, be courteous. Ask what they're calling about and do your best to get them to the right person or department. Speak calmly and politely and put a little warmth into your voice. Making callers feel that they matter goes a long way in establishing rapport and producing positive outcomes (see Chapter 5 for more about the essential skill of establishing rapport).

When the called person is out of the office or can't take the call, respond in one of the ways in Table 13-1 to protect the privacy of the other person and sound tactful. At the end of your comment, always ask whether the caller wants to leave a message on the person's voice mail.

Table 13-1   Tactful Responses when Colleagues
Can't Come to the Phone

What You Mean	What You Say
He's been out for the past two hours.	He's not in the office at the moment.
I don't know where she is. . . again.	She's stepped out of the office for a moment.
She's in the ladies room fixing her makeup.	She's stepped out of the office for a moment.
He's at his children's sports day.	He's out of the office today. May someone else help you?
She's having an argument with her boss.	She's unavailable at the moment.
He hasn't come in yet.	I expect him shortly.
She's busy.	She's unavailable at the moment.

Always address callers by name (as in 'Good afternoon Mr Jeffery', 'Good morning Mrs Wallace'). Never address callers you don't know by their first name.

Responding to callers' needs

Listen to callers and what they have to say. When you take a message, repeat back the information to confirm that you heard and took down the message correctly. I talk more about how to listen effectively in Chapter 4.

Be patient and helpful. Sometimes people call with a complaint and just want to vent their frustration. Whatever you do, don't snap back or speak rudely to the caller.

Never interject swear words, say anything disparaging or slam the receiver down while the other person is speaking. Doing so only escalates the problem.

Putting people on hold

Ideally don't put someone on hold, but if you absolutely have to, inform them politely first. Being put on hold can be a timewaster, especially if the person's thought process is being disturbed by Muzak intended to calm and divert callers' attention.

Do your best not to leave callers on hold for more than a few seconds or they may become upset and hang up.

Listening with Care and Enthusiasm

Always focus on a phone call and avoid being distracted by people and things around you. If someone tries to interrupt you, politely place your hand over the mouthpiece – or press the mute button – and point out that you're on a call and will speak with the person as soon as you're finished.

If the caller is rude or impatient, remain calm, diplomatic and polite. You're not the cause of their upset and so don't turn yourself into part of the problem. Show willingness and put yourself in the caller's shoes. By showing care and concern, you demonstrate that you value the person at the other end of the line.

When you're the cause of someone's upset accept responsibility and let the person know what you're going to do about it. Don't go into long explanations as to why you failed because that only causes more annoyance and no one cares about your lame excuses, no matter how innovative they may be. Apologise and let the other person know what you're going to do and by when. Once the problem is rectified, call the person to confirm and ask if there's anything else you can do to help. No matter how angry the other person may be, you must not demonstrate anything other than willingness to help resolve the problem. For more about listening and responding appropriately, flip to Chapter 4.

Putting a smile in your voice

When you're speaking on the phone people form opinions about you based on the way you sound. Research indicates that as much as 84 per cent of the judgements people form about the other person at the end of the line are based on the speaker's tone of voice. In other words, people can hear your personality through your voice. Therefore, even when you're feeling tired and out of sorts, you don't want your negativity to come through when you're on the phone with customers and colleagues. Your clients may misinterpret the stress in your voice as rudeness and take their business elsewhere.

No matter how carefully you choose your words, your tone of voice reveals your true emotions. Because this voice tone is closely linked to your facial expression, smile while you're talking. A smile warms up your voice, making it sound friendly, engaging and interested, and an enthusiastic voice is compelling and draws people to you.

Confirming your understanding

You build customer confidence when you take the time to confirm your understanding of a conversation or discussion. Crystallising what's been said and agreed creates an opportunity for you to correct misunderstandings and show good faith.

You can confirm your understanding by:

- ✔ **Using confirming statements.** Phrases such as 'Let me make sure I understand you. . .' or 'Let me repeat this back to you. . .' assure callers that they've successfully communicated what they intended.

- ✔ **Summarising key points.** When you review your understanding of the critical issues, you build agreement about the situation and shared values. At this point customers are able to express any further facts or needs they may have overlooked as well as variables that may influence their decisions. Here you can say, 'What I understand from our conversation is. . .' or 'So, to summarise. . .'.

- ✔ **Asking whether you understand correctly.** Checking to make sure that you understand what the caller wants to tell you gives them the opportunity to clarify any points or offer more information. Expressions you can use include, 'Have I missed anything?' and 'Do I understand that you. . .?'.

- ✔ **Clarifying misunderstandings if necessary and confirming new understanding.** When a point is clarified or new information introduced, reflect what you've heard and incorporate the details into your new understanding. Instead of callers feeling like they're talking to someone who doesn't understand them, you reduce tension by making them feel appreciated and valued. Two useful expressions in this context are 'From what you've said, I now understand that. . .' and 'I see, it's not. . . it's actually. . .'.

Closing the Call

No doubt you've been in the situation where at the end of the call the other person is long-winded, struggles to get to the point or doesn't seem to want to stop talking. In these situations ending the call becomes the challenge of the day. Whether you're closing the call with a customer, your dear old auntie Barbara or a talkative friend, I suggest that your default position is polite and assertive.

Begin by thanking such callers for their time and input. People like to feel validated and thanking them is one way of showing your respect and appreciation. In addition, when you thank people for their call, you're indicating that the call is now over. In a work setting, the following phrases are firm but polite ways of ending the call:

- ✔ 'Thank you for taking the time to talk this through. I really appreciate your feedback and suggestions.'

- ✔ 'Thank you for your input. I'll get back to you as soon as I have more information.'

In a more informal setting, saying 'I've taken up enough of your time' or 'This call must be costing you a fortune' are other ways of letting the person know that the time has come to stop the conversation.

Before hanging up, make sure that you're both in agreement about what's to happen next. When you summarise the agreed course of action with a definite 'do by' date you bring the discussion to a close with a clear understanding of the next steps (flip to the section 'Confirming your understanding' earlier in this chapter for more).

Just as important as making a great initial impression (as I discuss in the earlier section 'Managing the opening efficiently') is leaving callers with an excellent final one. As my ballet teacher told me many years ago, just before I went on stage for an audition, 'Start off strong and finish strong. What happens in the middle, they won't remember.'

Chapter 14

Putting Pen to Paper
for Positive Effect

....

In This Chapter

▶ Knowing the basics

▶ Writing great personal letters

▶ Sticking to business protocols

....

*A*lthough some people think that letter-writing has been relegated to history in favour of email, voice mail and texting, a place still exists for so-called snail mail. Whether you're sending a formal invitation, thanking your host for hospitality, conveying a message of congratulations or extending sympathy, nothing fits the bill better than a letter. In addition, knowing how to write proper business letters is a required skill.

In this chapter I provide plenty of information to keep in mind when communicating with the written word, for personal and professional correspondence.

Re-Introducing the Art of Letter-Writing

For business correspondence, the guidance I provide in this section is essential to make sure that you say what you want to and get that all-important appropriate tone for your message. Even for informal personal letters, observing these basic rules is sensible.

Keeping the recipient in mind

When writing a letter bear in mind the addressee. Consider what the person needs to know and take into account their expectations when opening your letter. For business and personal letters get to the point and don't bog your readers down with unnecessary information that has no relevance for them. While you can write as much as you like in a personal letter, make sure that the stories you tell, and the people, places and topics you write about, have interest and meaning for your reader. Your readers expect to read about your interests, exploits and any gossip you may want to share with them in a personal letter.

For business correspondence, limit your letter to a maximum of four paragraphs and, ideally, keep your content to one page. Your first paragraph should be short and state the purpose of your letter. The middle of your letter should contain relevant information behind your writing the letter. Keep the information to the essentials and organise your points in a clear and logical manner. In your last paragraph, state the action you expect the recipient to take, for example, offering you a refund, sending you further information or agreeing to a meeting.

Proofreading and revising before sending

When you write a letter, initially produce a draft to check for errors. Doing so helps to avoid the annoying experience of leaving out an important point or making spelling mistakes in a letter meant to create a positive impact.

Remember that business letters are a direct representation of you and, by extension, the organisation you work for. Make sure that your spelling and grammar are spot on – obvious errors in language look sloppy and unprofessional. Such faults mean that readers are justified in dismissing you and your organisation as lacking attention to detail and possessing below-par standards.

After writing your first draft, read the letter out loud. When you hear what you've written you can tell whether your message sounds right or not.

Getting Your Personal Letters Right

When you're writing to friends and family members you write in an informal manner. Addressing the recipient as 'Dear' is best for family members and letters with a serious tone. If you're writing to close friends you may want to start off with a simple 'Hi', 'Hey' or 'Hello'. Whatever greeting you choose, consider your recipient's personality and how the person likes to be addressed.

In this section I help you write some particular kinds of personal correspondence that people often find tricky.

Composing a condolence letter

Letters of condolence offer comfort to the grieving and let people know that you're thinking of them during their time of loss and sorrow. I prefer personal letters to mass-produced condolence cards. Taking the time to write words from your heart, acknowledging the deceased in terms of what that individual meant to you, is much more meaningful than off-the-shelf phrasing.

If you must turn to a shop-bought card, add a personal note on a separate piece of stationery and tuck it inside the card.

Write and send a sympathy letter promptly, waiting no more than two weeks after the loss. Produce a handwritten note on stationery, as opposed to typing and printing one from your computer. Also, avoid sounding fancy or formal: stick to your own voice and write to people the way you'd speak to them.

Follow the list of components below, in order, to guide you in writing a letter that serves as a tribute to the deceased and offers comfort to the bereaved:

1. **Acknowledge the loss and refer to the person by name.**

2. **Express your condolences.**

3. **Comment on the deceased's qualities that have particular meaning for you.**

4. **Include a favourite memory or story about the deceased.**

5. **Offer help only if you intend to follow through.**

6. **End your letter with a special expression of sympathy or a thoughtful wish.** Usual endings ('Love', 'Sincerely' or 'Best wishes') can sound a bit impersonal. Perhaps write 'You're in my thoughts and prayers during this time of loss and reflection'.

Jotting an invitation

According to Debrett's, the arbiter of social etiquette, good taste and proper behaviour (see www.debretts.com/etiquette/communication/written/invitations.aspx), you should write formal invitations to parties at your home on white or cream high-quality cards (commonly called *at Home* cards). The card should measure 15 x 11.5 centimetres (6 x 4.5 inches) and the heavier the card, the more elegant it is. The best ones are engraved, though you can avoid the added expenditure by using raised printing *(thermography)*.

A typical at Home card has the hostess's name centred near the top with the words 'at Home' beneath. (In a hangover from the 19th century, the person extending the invitation is traditionally the female in the family.) Handwritten below – in black or blue fountain pen – are the details of the event, such as 'for lunch' or 'for dinner', followed by the date and time. At the bottom left of the card is the address, identified for replying by 'R.S.V.P'. In the upper left corner, again handwritten, are the first names of the people you're inviting. If you're inviting one person plus another, write 'Name of Invitee and Guest'. This frightfully posh form of social shorthand eliminates the wordiness that can clutter up a smart invitation.

If at Home cards seem a bit much for your taste, write a simple note along the lines of:

Dear Nicky,

Karl and I would be delighted if you and Thomas could join us for dinner at our house on Saturday, 7 March at 7:30 p.m. Please respond to the address below and let us know of any allergies or special dietary requests. Dress: jacket, no tie. Looking forward to seeing you both soon.

Sending a thank-you note

Although people don't give gifts, do favours or invite you to a weekend stay at their manor house in the country (lucky you!) with the intention of receiving a thank-you note, they appreciate the letters when they come. Manners dictate that when someone offers you hospitality or kindness in any form, a simple note of thanks is required.

People like being appreciated and knowing that you value their kindness. Whether you liked the gift or enjoyed the dinner party doesn't matter. Every offering deserves a note of thanks. Even the hand-crocheted Christmas sweater with the winking Santa on the front requires an appreciative acknowledgement.

Here's a simple formula for writing a thank-you letter:

1. **Greet the giver, as in 'Dear Aunt Paula'.** According to Dale Carnegie and Direct Marketers, people like hearing the sound of their names and reading them in print. No matter how poor your penmanship, your note needs to be handwritten, preferably in blue or black ink, and not using a whimsical marking pen.

2. **Express your gratitude, as in 'Thank you so much for the cashmere scarf. . .'.** Avoid expressions that state the obvious, such as 'I'm just writing to say. . .'. Write in the present tense to indicate that what you're saying is happening in the here and now.

3. **Never mention money.** Replace any reference to finances with the words 'your generosity' or 'your kindness'. The same goes for an intangible gift, such as putting you up for the weekend. In this case, you'd write, 'Thank you for your kind hospitality.' Simple phrasing is fine, because what you're doing is creating a simple expression of sincere appreciation.

4. **Discuss the use of a gift.** Writing something complimentary about the gift and how you plan to use it such as, 'I'll think of you when I wrap up against the cold this winter,' makes givers feel that their efforts hit the spot. If the gift was time spent in someone's home, you can write 'I appreciated getting to know you and your family and how welcome you made me feel.' If the gift was money, allude to how you can use it, such as,

'Your generous gift will be a great help in decorating my apartment.'

5. **Refer to the past, allude to the future.** Write along the lines of, 'I love that you made the effort to join us at Christmas and look forward to seeing you at Mum's birthday in the spring.' You add value to a relationship by telling givers how they fit into the pattern of your life. If you don't see the giver often, refer to something positive that's happening in that person's life.

6. **Give final thanks.** Acknowledging the gift a final time ties up your letter nicely.

7. **Sign off.** Wrap up your note as you prefer. A simple 'Love', 'Fondly' or 'Warmest regards' above your signature is ideal. Pop it in the post no more than ten days after the gift was given.

Crafting Successful Business Correspondence

Letters play a significant role in business, with clarity, focus and brevity being the central requirements for capturing and holding your reader's attention. As well as providing general advice, I also talk you through some particular business letters that you're sure to need at some point in your career.

Chatty, casual language is best left to your personal letters. No matter how well you know the reader, when your letter is on company letterhead your words take on a professional tone, meaning and, crucially, consequences.

Keeping your letters concise

Long, rambling letters have no place in today's busy business world. Respect your addressee's time by keeping your letters concise, factual and focused. Limit yourself to one page or your reader may throw your letter straight into the nearest waste bin (and everyone knows the enjoyment of dunking a crumpled letter, basketball-style).

Before writing a business letter, determine your aim: ask your-self why you're writing and what you want to achieve. The clearer you are in your own mind about your goal, the better you can phrase your letter. By focusing on including informa-tion that supports your aim and deleting the irrelevant, you're able to keep to the subject in a clear, concise way.

A business letter comprises three parts:

- **Introduction:** Telling your recipient your reason for writ-ing allows you to set the context for them to consider your comments. Examples of reasons for writing include requesting a job interview, making a complaint or offering a business opportunity.

- **Specifics:** These are what you want to accomplish. Here you lay out the goal for your letter.

- **Conclusion and recommendations:** Here you state what you want to happen next. Make yourself clear about what you desire from the other person and what you're going to do.

In a one-page A4 letter, use no more than three or four para-graphs to convey your message. Make the paragraph lines single spaced, with a double space between each paragraph. A typical letter page holds 350–450 words.

Sticking to the point

Make your reason for writing clear from the beginning. Of course you want to sound friendly in your letters, but you also want to appear efficient. Don't leave your reader wondering about the point of your letter.

If you need to ask a question, do so directly. For example, instead of writing, 'We would appreciate hearing from you to confirm whether you want to maintain or change your current level of service plan,' ask 'Do you want to continue with your current plan or change it?'

Close your business letters with a call to action, stating what you'd like the reader to do and how you're going to follow up.

Jettisoning the jargon

Although jargon and its cousins – abbreviated terminology, acronyms, contractions and other forms of gobbledygook – can be efficient shortcuts, they also confuse readers unfamiliar with your industry. Avoid jargon if you want your letter to be read.

Also, readers can become frustrated with 'inside speak', which increases the risk of them disregarding your message. Jargon causes misunderstandings and creates barriers to clear communication by making your recipients feel out of the loop, if not completely stupid. After all, if you choose to rely on jargon to convey your message, your readers may conclude that they should understand what you're talking about. And making someone feel inadequate is certainly not conducive to getting the result you're after.

Fill your letters with acronyms, abbreviations and other forms of jargon only if you don't care whether or not your reader understands your message.

Writing specific official letters

From time to time you need to write specific career or professional letters, such as an application for your dream job or even your resignation. In this section I guide you through a few common, but often tricky, examples.

Composing a letter of interest

When you want to work for a particular company, you write a *letter of interest*. Sounds simple, except that for a letter to stand out from the crowd you need to have style, an appropriate tone and sell your strengths all on one page. Your letter of interest may be the first contact your potential employer has with you, and so you want to make sure that your letter:

✔ Convinces the employer that you're the best person for the job.

✔ Entices the employer to read your CV.

✔ Makes the employer want to interview you.

Here are some hints to make your letter stand out:

- ✔ **Address your letter to the individual who's hiring.** If in doubt, call the company and find out.

- ✔ **Research the company.** Match your strengths to the needs of the job to which you're applying. Doing so demonstrates that you're eager to contribute to the success of the organisation.

- ✔ **Stick to one page.** Make sure to refer to specific points in your CV.

- ✔ **Structure your letter in the following order:**

  1. **In your first paragraph, state why you're applying for the position,** how you became familiar with the company and why you want to work for it.

  2. **In the next paragraph, highlight how you can contribute to the company's success.** Include your education, experiences and accomplishments as well as your strengths and positive personal characteristics. Refer to your CV and other relevant documents.

  3. **In your final paragraph, express your desire to meet with the reader and discuss your potential role in the company.** Offer a specific date and time when you'll call to arrange a follow-up.

  4. **Close your letter with a cordial sign off –** 'Sincerely' or 'Thank you' – and add your signature above your typed name.

Creating a CV cover letter

A cover letter accompanies and fleshes out the details of your CV. In it you point out your qualities that make you an outstanding candidate for the job and which give a personal statement about you as an individual. View your covering letter as the personal touch to your CV.

Stick to one page, keep your letter easy to read, write actively rather than passively (that is, write along the lines of 'I want to work for your company' and not 'I would like you to employ me') and answer the question, 'Why should I see you?' As in your letter of interest (see the preceding section) include your understanding of the company, why you want to pursue this particular career and how your qualities and experience make you the ideal candidate. Also let the reader know when you're available to start.

Resigning in writing

When you resign from your job, do so with dignity and graciousness. The notice period depends on individual job contracts, but give your employer adequate notice so that you don't leave them in a difficult situation, provide thanks for the opportunities they've given you and leave on a positive note.

To avoid the shock factor, tell your boss face to face that you're resigning and then follow up with a formal letter in which you explain why you're resigning and how you feel about it. Even if the reasons are negative, don't include any disparaging comments about any aspect of the company. Your letter will be placed in your employment file and so keep it polite and professional.

Consider the following points when writing your letter:

✔ **Include the fact that you're resigning and the date of your last day of work.** You may also thank your employer for your time at the organisation if you wish.

✔ **Keep it brief.** Don't go into lengthy explanations as to why you're resigning – unless you have a positive reason, such as relocating or changing careers – or give gory details if you've been unhappy in your job.

✔ **Offer your assistance.** Let your employer know that you're available to help out during the transition period. Provide a phone number and email address where you can be contacted.

No matter how unhappy you may have been in your job, don't scribble a note in rage and fling it at your manager as you storm out the door. Unless, of course, you don't care about your reputation or if you ever work again! Don't vent – blaming, accusing and casting aspersions make you look petty and small-minded. (Check out Chapter 6 for more about the negative effects of a bad attitude).

Providing a reference letter

Students, job applicants and prospective members of exclusive golf clubs, to mention just a few examples, require letters of recommendation. If someone asks you to write a reference, you need to be able to testify honestly to the person's character, skills and achievements.

A letter of recommendation is a formal document and so you must be truthful, or you face possible legal repercussions if your comments don't fit the candidate.

When writing a recommendation, consider if you're writing this as a 'personal' reference or if you're representing your company. If it's the latter, be sure to check your corporate HR policy or guidelines about writing a recommendation.

Start your letter in the basic business format, including addressing the recipient as 'Dear [name]' or 'To Whom It May Concern', and then adhere to these points:

1. **Introduce yourself.** Give a brief outline of your position and your relationship with the candidate.

2. **Confirm the details you know the candidate plans to supply along with your letter.** These may include the person's job title when working for you, role in the company, leaving salary and dates of employment.

3. **Supply your judgement about the candidate's suitability for the job, including specific skills and outstanding qualities.** You can single out any exceptional features, such as the person's enthusiasm, attention to detail or ability to lead.

4. **Offer concrete examples of where and when the candidate excelled.** You may want to discuss this point with the candidate in case the person wants you to include a specific example.

5. **Close your letter on a positive note.** Offer to provide further information if required and include your contact details.

End a letter to someone you know or a named recipient with 'Yours sincerely'. Otherwise, sign off with 'Yours faithfully'.

Sending thanks for an interview

Research from the York Technical Institute shows that less than 4 per cent of job applicants send thank-you letters after interviews. If you fail to write one, don't be surprised if you fail to get the job. Write promptly, within 24 hours of your interview, to everyone who interviewed you and all those who helped you with your job search.

If a group interviewed you and the interviews were very similar, a 'group' letter is fine. In this case address all the people on a master letter, adding a personal handwritten note to each. Of course, you may choose to send personal letters to each interviewer, which may take a little longer but shows extra effort on your part. If you forgot to say something in your interview, use the thank-you letter to bring it up. Keep your comments short and offer to elaborate in the future if the reader wants to know more. Structure your letter in four parts:

1. **A thank you for the interview.**

2. **An expression of your interest in the job.**

3. **A reminder of your qualifications and skills.**

4. **A final thank you for the interviewer's time and interest.**

When writing a thank-you note, keep your reader in mind. Although typed letters are easy to read, a handwritten note goes a long way in making a positive impression.

Sending a letter of farewell

When you write a farewell letter to a firm, you want to leave your reader with a final positive impression of you. Now is not the time to dump your gripes and grievances. Instead, write a goodbye to your colleagues and thank them for their support, guidance and encouragement during your time together.

Let them know that you've accepted a new job, are retiring or are moving on to new pastures (as appropriate) to curb the gossip-mongers. If you genuinely like the people you're writing to, ask if you can keep in touch and seek their advice if you need it in the future. Finally, provide them with your private contact details, but only if you want to hear from them.

Part VI
The Part of Tens

'Isn't it time we started to talk to each other again, Barbara?'

In this part...

*Y*ou know for sure you're reading a *For Dummies* book when you flip to the Part of Tens. In this section you get a quick rundown of simple tips and techniques for face-to-face communication, where your willingness to understand, your desire to connect and your ability to let go of the negative and embrace the positive all meet up. You also find basic tenets from childhood lessons that serve you well every time you apply them.

Chapter 15

Ten Top Tips for Speaking Face to Face

*I*f you want quick, easy and practical tips for getting your message across while you're speaking to someone, you've come to the right chapter! Whether you're talking to your lover, your mother or your employer, follow these simple guidelines and you're sure to communicate in a way that makes your listener hungry to hear what you have to say.

Minding Your Attitude

The most successful communicators understand the power of focused expectation. When you know how you want your listener to respond, you're able to guide the conversation in that direction. Of course, when other people are involved you can't be assured of getting what you want, but if you fail to believe that you even stand a chance, you definitely won't.

Your expectations often determine the result and so the first step is to believe you're going to get what you want.

Let go of judgements, blame and any other unconstructive thoughts. When you relegate negativity to the dustbin you're ready to open yourself to positive possibilities. People are drawn to and energised by positive attitudes. (Check out the later section 'Letting Go of Negativity' for more detail.)

To steer clear of communication barriers ask yourself, 'What has to happen to make this work?'. You can also step into the shoes of your listeners: see yourself through their eyes and hear how you communicate with them. Ask yourself whether you're making your proposition attractive to them.

Your thoughts affect your words, your words become actions, your actions become habits and your habits become character.

For more about how attitude impacts on communication, turn to Chapter 6.

Engaging with Your Eyes

Your eyes reveal your thoughts, attitudes and beliefs. Where you look when you're speaking and listening reveals how you feel about the subject or person you're engaging with. For example, if someone rolls their eyes after you make your point, they're letting you know that they see things differently. If they avoid making eye contact, you can bet they're hiding something from you.

In Western cultures, making eye contact during a conversation indicates that you're confident, trustworthy and honest. Lack of eye contact, however, indicates disinterest, dislike or disengagement.

In Eastern and some Caribbean cultures making direct eye contact is considered rude. For more about communication and cultural differences, have a look at Chapter 11.

Here are some tips to help discern the meaning behind someone's eyes:

✔ When a person is sexually interested in someone, their pupils dilate and their gaze lingers a little longer than normal with the other person.

✔ When arguing or making a point, people demonstrate their strength and commitment by looking the other person directly in the eye without breaking their gaze.

✔ When deferring to someone, people lower their eyes to indicate submissiveness.

Flip to Chapter 8 to pick up more hints on using your eyes.

Speaking Clearly

If you want your listener to understand what you're saying, know what you want to say before you open your mouth. (Skip to Chapter 2 for more about speaking with a clear intention.) Then, when you're clear about what you want to say, make sure that you can be understood. Remove the metaphorical marbles from your mouth and articulate:

- ✔ Concentrate on your consonants to make sure that you communicate what you really mean.

- ✔ Highlight your main points by emphasising key words.

- ✔ Speak slowly enough to be understood, and yet not so slowly as to put your audience to sleep.

- ✔ Engage with your listeners by lacing your sentences and phrases with appropriate words that hold meaning for them.

- ✔ Avoid overloading your message with too many points.

Chapter 7 is filled with further tips and techniques for clear speaking.

Putting Energy into Your Voice

Every day people judge you based on the sound of your voice: a dull and lifeless one indicates a dull and lifeless mind. Because your voice is the mechanism for projecting your personality and influencing others, you need to fill it with some get-up-and-go.

Standing with strong legs – in which your muscles are solid and sturdy rather than slack and relaxed – and a loose upper body provides you with power and freedom when communicating. Take a look at photos or film clips of Elvis Presley singing to see what I mean. If The King had relied on his neck and throat to provide energy to his voice, he'd never have produced the sound he did. Instead, he turned to the true source of power: a solid foundation and a relaxed upper body (though I don't recommend pelvic wriggling during board meetings!).

For more about energising your voice, read Chapter 7.

 For putting power into your lower body, imagine a flow of energy expanding downwards through your legs and feet into the ground beneath you, like the tap root of a giant oak. To avoid locking your knees, which would inhibit your movement, pretend that you have shallow roots, coming off the bottom of your feet, so that you can bend and sway like a willow tree.

Positioning Yourself for Best Effect

Unless you're the Wizard of Oz, Big Brother or the mysterious boss in *Charlie's Angels,* let your listeners see you to help them understand what you mean. If you're delivering a message that's clear and direct, look your listeners in the eye and position yourself right in front of them. If you want to indicate that you're uncertain or uncomfortable about what you're saying, slightly turn away.

 Lean forward as you speak to show that you're interested in the person you're speaking to and feel positive about what you're saying. Pull away to signal that you've disengaged.

You can find out more about how to position yourself to best advantage in my book *Body Language For Dummies* (Wiley) and by turning to Chapter 8.

Listening with Willingness

Whether at work or at home, listening with the desire to understand is critical to effective communication. Problems arise when people don't want to listen, usually because they disagree with what the speaker is saying or aren't interested. One of my favourite teachers told me, 'Listening is the willingness to change.'

When you really listen to what someone's saying, you're opening yourself up to being influenced or persuaded to a new way of thinking, feeling or behaving. When you listen with willingness you're indicating that you want to know more and be inspired.

Research shows that powerful people have such confidence in their opinions that changing their position is a difficult task – convinced of their own beliefs they struggle to be swayed. According to Pablo Brinol and Richard Petty, authors of an Ohio State University study, the best way to get leaders to listen is to put them in a situation where they don't feel as powerful.

Check out Chapter 4 for more about listening skills.

Letting Go of Negativity

Negativity is malignant and infectious. It drains energy, pollutes minds, decreases enthusiasm and creativity and harms performance and productivity. Not to mention the fact that negative people are tedious and tiresome to talk to.

Blaming and complaining during conversations are sure ways to push people away: anger, bitterness and resentment open the door to loneliness. Unless you want to live a fearful, critical and judgemental life filled with discomfort and adversity, let go of the negativity and focus your energy on situations you can influence and change.

Negativity has an adverse effect on your health, wellbeing and job performance.

Chapter 6 talks about out how your attitude influences your communications.

Feeding Back What You Hear

When you demonstrate that you've heard what people have said and mean, they're willing to walk across hot coals for you. Restating or paraphrasing what you hear shows that you grasp their picture and get their message, making them feel understood and cared about and letting them know they matter.

Feeding back what you hear helps establish a common ground between you and the other person. You're letting them know that, rather than making assumptions or judging their opinions, you're interested in understanding their point of view.

Listening attentively allows you not only to feed back the other person's words, but also helps you pick up on the feelings and emotions behind what's been said.

The next time you're communicating with someone, practise the following steps:

1. **Paraphrase what you hear.** Offer a concise statement of the speaker's message, focusing on the facts or ideas.

2. **Reflect the feeling behind the message.** Silently ask yourself, 'How would I feel if I were having that experience?', and then restate the feeling in a way that conveys your understanding.

3. **Summarise the speaker's main ideas and feelings to show understanding.** Doing so displays that you've grasped the message and gives the person a chance to gain a full picture of what's been communicated.

Chapter 4 provides you with lots of ways of letting people know that you've really heard them.

Paying Attention to Body Language

How people move their muscles demonstrates their attitudes, feelings and emotions. For example, drumming fingers, tapping feet and audible sighs can indicate annoyance, boredom or frustration.

Take notice of how you move your body when speaking with someone you like. Chances are that you lean towards the person, smile and let your eyes linger longer than usual. Conversely, if you don't like someone you tend to pull away, avoid eye contact and put as much distance between yourselves as you possibly can.

Hesitant movements, hunched shoulders and a dropping head indicate subservience, doubt and insecurity whereas touching, expansive gestures and a radiant smile indicate dominance and say 'I'm in control.'

Accurately reading body language requires you to pay attention to a cluster of gestures and expressions, not just movement. You can pick up some tips on how to do it by flipping to Chapter 8.

Minding Your Tone of Voice

Your voice tone plays a major part in conveying your message and affects how people respond to you. If you speak in an upbeat way and your voice is warm, clear and in control, you come across as knowledgeable and confident. If your voice is harsh, hesitant or hard to hear, people don't want to listen.

Deep voices have more credibility than high-pitched ones, which are better left for conveying excitement and enthusiasm. Curt, harsh and loud voices can illustrate anger whereas soft murmurs and soothing tones reflect pleasure or contentment.

If your tone rises in pitch at the end of your sentences you sound like you're asking a question or requesting permission. Also, a tone that's stuck in your nose like Janice's in the comedy *Friends* is just irritating! So aim to drop the pitch of your voice at the end of your sentence when making a point or statement.

Discover more about voice tone in Chapter 7 and in *Voice & Speaking Skills For Dummies* by Judy Apps (Wiley).

Chapter 16

Ten Essential Tips for Effective Communication

In This Chapter

▶ Observing before speaking

▶ Caring enough to get it right

*H*ere's an important fact to remember – you can never not communicate. Or, to put it another way, you're always going to disclose, pass on or reveal something. Whether you're speaking faster than the speed of sound or not saying a word, you're communicating. The tips in this chapter help you to communicate clearly and so take control of what you want to convey. You can then be confident that you've made yourself understood and in turn have understood others.

Treating the Other Person with Respect

When you treat people with respect you can count on them returning the favour, or at least appreciating your efforts. Most people want to be treated with respect, dignity and courtesy. Throw in a little politeness and kindness and you're onto a winner.

Some ways you can treat others with respect include:

✔ Encouraging people to express their ideas and opinions.

✔ Letting others finish making their points before interjecting yours.

✔ Never insulting, disparaging or putting down people or their points of view.

✔ Praising more frequently than you criticise, and when you do criticise, focusing on the behaviour and not the person.

✔ Implementing the Platinum Rule: treat people the way they want to be treated.

Turn to Chapter 5 for more about the value of treating people with respect.

Knowing the Preferred Form of Communication

The best communicators know how to engage with people in ways that they can understand and are comfortable with. Here are some common preferences to watch out for:

✔ Some people like to talk while they think and others prefer silence as they organise their thoughts.

✔ Some people like to focus on fine detail and practical applications, and others are comfortable speaking about concepts and possibilities.

✔ Some people like to communicate through the written word and others like to pick up the phone or talk face to face.

Whichever form your counterpart prefers, if you want to open up the lines of communication, adapt your style to meet theirs. (Find out more about communication and technology in Chapter 12.)

A 2009 survey in *Success* magazine asked 950 professional people, 'What is your preferred method of communicating?' The following results are worth bearing in mind when weighing up the likelihood of someone's preference:

✔ 3 per cent: text messaging

✔ 5 per cent: social media

✔ 13 per cent: telephone

✔ 39 per cent: face to face

✔ 40 per cent: email

The *Success* magazine survey showed that 89 per cent of the respondents have a college education compared to the national index of 60.7 per cent. 53 per cent are self-employed compared to the national index of 6.4 per cent and the mean household income is $126,300 compared to the national index of $73,600. The respondents who prefer communication by email do so for time management reasons. They don't like being interrupted unless it's urgent and they are most productive when they can write and respond to their emails in scheduled blocks of time.

For those who like to talk on the phone, call them. For those who like to see the person they're talking to, arrange a face-to-face meeting. Whatever the other person's favoured form, if building relationships and communicating effectively matters to you, revert to the other person's preference. After you develop a compatible communication relationship, you can slowly transition people to using your chosen style.

For more about understanding how people prefer to communicate, flip to Chapter 3.

Thinking Before You Speak

When I was a child I was taught to 'Stop. Look. Listen.' Only after adhering to that instruction was I allowed to speak. If you've ever said something on the spur of the moment you later regret, you know the value of this lesson.

Frequently, when you find yourself reacting quickly in stressful or confrontational situations, words can spurt forth from your mouth before your brain has time to consider your response. That's fine when you need to issue an immediate warning ('Fire!') but not so great when afterwards you rue the outburst ('You idiot!').

The next time you're tempted to blurt out what's on your mind, pause and consider the information you're about to share. If your words are respectful, clarify a situation or provide value, speak away. If not, keep your mouth shut. Speak only if your comments are:

- ✔ Accurate
- ✔ Appropriate

✔ Effective

✔ Necessary

✔ Timely

As Thomas Jefferson said, 'When angry, count to ten before you speak. If very angry, count to one hundred.'

Talking Less and Listening More

You have two ears, two eyes and one mouth, and so use them in that order. By observing more than talking, you gain useful information that you can refer to at appropriate times. (In Chapter 4, I explore the value of listening to understand.)

When you're listening, give the speaker your complete and focused attention. Confirm your understanding by rephrasing pertinent points, and avoid interrupting. Acknowledge points with appropriate body language, such as nodding for understanding, mirroring the speaker's movements to create rapport and maintaining eye contact to show that you're paying attention. (For more about mirroring posture and energy for creating rapport, check out Chapter 5).

Asking Questions to Understand

Expert communicators are interested in what others have to say. They care about people and participate in conversations. Asking questions helps you gain information, clarify and verify what you've heard, check your understanding and demonstrate to others a level of interest.

At work people are frequently assigned to projects or tasks that don't really interest them. They also may not have a sufficient amount of experience, information or expertise to complete the project successfully. When you're allocating work, ask questions like, 'I know this isn't your area of expertise, so what can I do to help you?' or 'What do you find interesting about being part of this project?' You can also ask a question that has specialist knowledge aspects within it to check for the other person's level of skill or expertise. The more you ask, the more you find out. Turn to Chapter 4 to discover more about understanding.

Asking open questions that begin with 'what', 'how', 'when', 'who' and 'where' elicits more information than closed questioning, which usually receives a single word or short, factual answer. Open questions are good for finding out detail whereas closed questions are good for confirming understanding, concluding a discussion or making a decision. I write about asking questions in Chapter 9.

Minding Your Non-Verbal Behaviour

Your facial expressions, gestures and posture as well as your tone of voice, appearance and the distance you put between yourself and others all impact on communication. For example:

✔ How you use your eye gaze can indicate a range of emotions from hostility to interest and attraction. For example, staring with a frown and contracted eyes looks antagonistic, aggressive or just plain unfriendly, while widening your eyes and raising your eyebrows can make you appear submissive, so be careful about holding someone's stare in an inappropriate way. Similarly, lack of eye contact can indicate your boredom, embarrassment or discomfort. With a simple touch you can communicate affection, familiarity and sympathy.

✔ Be aware that a slouched posture indicates your disengagement, whereas leaning back in your chair looking to the ceiling makes you appear to be deep in thought. Turn to Chapter 8 for more about how you can communicate through your movements.

✔ Your tone of voice, inflection, pace and pitch influence how your message is received. To seek approval or passion, speak in a strong tone of voice. To indicate lack of interest or disapproval, say the same words in a hesitant way. Pick up more information about the power of the voice in Chapter 7.

Handling Disagreements with Diplomacy

When you live and work with people you're bound to disagree at some point. Disagreements stem from differing points of view and aren't inherently detrimental. Handled well, conflict can clear the air and revitalise a relationship. When handled badly or simply ignored, however, conflict can lead to negative feelings and behaviours.

The general guidelines in the following list help to bring harmony to a potentially volatile situation:

- **Reflect your understanding of the other person's view or opinion.** Saying 'What I'm hearing you say is. . .' lets others know that you're listening to their opinions and taking them into consideration before expressing yours.

- **Acknowledge that you value the other people as individuals despite having different opinions.** Communicate that you respect their opinion by saying, as appropriate, 'I understand (appreciate, respect, see how you feel that way and so on).'

- **State your position or opinion.** By letting others know what you want, feel or think, you show that, although you don't agree with them, you value your relationship and are looking to exchange ideas, not create conflict.

For more details about dealing with conflict and difficult situations, see Chapter 9.

Opening Yourself to New Ideas

Although you've probably been raised with a set of beliefs and values that inform your decisions, the same is true for other people, even those whose beliefs and values differ from yours. This fact doesn't mean that you're right and they're wrong; you're just different. By opening yourself to other points of view, you can reap rewards that lead to:

- Making more informed decisions.
- Increasing your personal creativity.

✔ Developing certainty, clarity and confidence about your own position.

The British philosopher John Stuart Mill argued that being open to new ideas allows you to reaffirm your beliefs with greater confidence. After all, an unconsidered idea lacks justification. When you seriously consider new ideas you may discover solid reasons for believing what you do.

Opening yourself to new ideas also increases the likelihood of developing your creativity. Even if a new idea itself isn't useful, compelling or perfect, merely considering issues from a different point of view can change your way of thinking about various subjects, enhancing your own problem-solving skills. In addition, you just may discover novel solutions that you hadn't considered.

No one likes people who refuse to listen and insist on being right. By opening yourself to others' opinions and alternative arguments, you open the door to new partnerships and possible friendships.

In Chapter 3, I take a look at some of the different ways people communicate that can help you see the value of diverse points of view.

Following Through on Promises

Although making a promise can help people feel good in the moment, if you fail to follow through you let others down, damage your reputation and can make matters worse for the person you promised. When you give your word, people place their trust in you, counting on you to be trustworthy and dependable. So never make a promise if you lack the intention to live up to it.

The following steps can help you fulfil your promises:

1. **Ask yourself whether you can imagine doing what you're thinking about promising.** If you can, prepare to deliver. If you can't, don't make the promise or even present the possibility.

2. **Determine how long you're going to take to deliver.** Don't tell the other person your timeframe at this

point, because if you can't match your expectations, you end up looking untrustworthy.

3. **Break a complex task into bite-sized chunks.** In this way, you can work through it one step at a time.

4. **Find a way to over-deliver on your promise after you complete the task.** When you tip the scales in your favour, you enhance your reputation.

Value isn't found in making promises. Value is found in delivering promises.

Recognising What's Going On Beneath the Surface

If you want to communicate effectively, remember that feelings and emotions lie beneath the spoken word. Whether someone is feeling sad, stressed, joyous or abused, the emotion is going to impact on the communication.

Sometimes people suppress their emotions, causing them to pretend that something doesn't matter, when it really does. They may blow up over minor incidents, talk about interests rather than personal matters and feelings, or not talk at all. Lethargy, fatigue and depression may colour their conversation. In Chapter 4, I offer you ways of listening to help you understand how someone is really feeling.

All humans are complex characters, and so they don't always recognise that they – and others – are experiencing emotions that they're expressing through the way they're speaking and behaving, rather than addressing their emotions out loud. They may recognise that something seems peculiar, wrong or simply 'off' and yet are unable to identify what the problem is, or if one even exists.

If you remember nothing else from what you read in this book, remember to listen to others with the intention to understand. Only by giving people your time and undivided attention can you create clear, effective communication. Be curious!

Index

About the Author

Elizabeth Kuhnke is an Executive Presence Coach who works with people struggling to present themselves at their authentic best. She's highly experienced in helping clients to reflect on beliefs and behaviours that may be holding them back from achieving what they want. Her outstanding ability to build trust, rapport and a relaxed working environment enables her clients to make quick progress towards stated goals.

As a successful author for the international bestselling *For Dummies* series, having written *Body Language*, *Persuasion & Influence*, and *Communication Skills* for the brand, Elizabeth is expert in understanding listeners' needs and communicating clearly, concisely and compellingly. An accomplished actress in the USA, she is also a qualified Neuro-Linguistic Programming Practitioner, an accredited Myers Briggs Type Indicator Administrator and holds advanced degrees in Speech and Communications. She regularly participates in continuous professional development and holds several coaching qualifications.

Since starting her business, Elizabeth has worked mainly with individuals and groups at a senior level, primarily in FTSE 100 and Fortune 500 companies as well as the charity sector. She frequently appears in the media commenting on non-verbal behaviour. She is also the recipient of a Sue Ryder Women of Achievement Award.

Author's Acknowledgements

When the *For Dummies* team offered me the opportunity
to write this book, I was thrilled. Clear, credible, and connected communication is one of my passions, and to have the
opportunity to further my knowledge and share insights and
information with you was a proposition that I couldn't refuse.
In addition, knowing that I would be supported by the incredible team of talented, committed, and experienced editors,
lead by Kerry, Erica and Andy, sealed the deal.

The content of this book is based on more than twenty years
of learning about and practising the art and science of successful communication. To my dedicated teachers and amazing clients, I respect and value each one of you and thank you
for offering me the chance to do what I love and learn in the
process.

To my colleagues, especially Kate, Wanda, Annie and Sue,
thank you for your wisdom, your generosity, and your collaboration. To Liz Wallace, John Lucy and Nick Jeffery, thank
you for your endorsements, your backing and your constant
belief in my abilities.

To Charlotte, your cheeriness, competency and consideration enable me to perform at my best and without you, Tom,
the business wouldn't be here.

To Karl, Kristina, and Max, your love and support keep me
going. I shudder to think where I'd be without you. To Henry,
a dear friend and loyal companion, who sadly died just
before publication, this one's for you.

Finally, my sincere thanks to the thousands of readers who
have bought my books. It's my wish that you gain useful
knowledge, put it to practice and have fun in the process.
Please accept this closing thought from a fellow coach as my
gift to you, 'The way you communicate with others and with
yourself, determines the quality of your life.'

Publisher's Acknowledgements

We're proud of this book; please send us your comments at http://dummies.
custhelp.com. For other comments, please contact our Customer Care
Department within the U.S. at 877-762-2974, outside the U.S. at (001) 317-572-3993,
or fax 317-572-4002.

Some of the people who helped bring this book to market include the following:

Acquisitions, Editorial, and Vertical Websites

Commissioning Editor: Kerry Laudon

Project Editor: Erica Peters

Assistant Editor: Ben Kemble

Development Editor: Andy Finch

Technical Reviewer: Kate Rees

Copy Editor: Martin Key

Proofreader: Helen Heyes

Production Manager: Daniel Mersey

Publisher: Miles Kendall

Cover Photo: © Peter Booth / iStock

Cartoons: Ed McLachlan

Composition Services

Senior Project Coordinator: Kristie Rees

Indexer: BIM Indexing & Proofreading Services

FOR DUMMIES

Making Everything Easier!™

UK editions

BUSINESS

Bookkeeping
FOR DUMMIES
978-0-470-97626-5

Persuasion & Influence
FOR DUMMIES
978-0-470-74737-7

Starting & Running a Business
ALL-IN-ONE
FOR DUMMIES
978-1-119-97527-4

REFERENCE

British Politics
FOR DUMMIES
978-0-470-68637-9

DIY
FOR DUMMIES
978-0-470-97450-6

Dad's Guide to Pregnancy
FOR DUMMIES
978-1-119-97660-8

HOBBIES

Growing Your Own Fruit & Veg
FOR DUMMIES
978-0-470-69960-7

Keeping Chickens
FOR DUMMIES
978-1-119-99417-6

Beekeeping
FOR DUMMIES
978-1-119-97250-1

Asperger's Syndrome For Dummies
978-0-470-66087-4

Basic Maths For Dummies
978-1-119-97452-9

Body Language For Dummies,
2nd Edition
978-1-119-95351-7

Boosting Self-Esteem For Dummies
978-0-470-74193-1

British Sign Language For Dummies
978-0-470-69477-0

Cricket For Dummies
978-0-470-03454-5

Diabetes For Dummies, 3rd Edition
978-0-470-97711-8

Electronics For Dummies
978-0-470-68178-7

English Grammar For Dummies
978-0-470-05752-0

Flirting For Dummies
978-0-470-74259-4

IBS For Dummies
978-0-470-51737-6

Improving Your Relationship
For Dummies
978-0-470-68472-6

ITIL For Dummies
978-1-119-95013-4

Management For Dummies,
2nd Edition
978-0-470-97769-9

Neuro-linguistic Programming
For Dummies, 2nd Edition
978-0-470-66543-5

Nutrition For Dummies, 2nd Edition
978-0-470-97276-2

Organic Gardening For Dummies
978-1-119-97706-3

Making Everything Easier! ™

UK editions

SELF-HELP

Cognitive Behavioural Therapy For Dummies
978-0-470-66541-1

Creative Visualization For Dummies
978-1-119-99264-6

Mindfulness For Dummies
978-0-470-66086-7

STUDENTS

Philosophy For Dummies
978-0-470-68820-5

Student Cookbook For Dummies
978-0-470-974711-7

Sociology For Dummies
978-1-119-99134-2

HISTORY

The Tudors For Dummies
978-0-470-68792-5

Medieval History For Dummies
978-0-470-74783-4

British History For Dummies
978-0-470-97819-1

Origami Kit For Dummies
978-0-470-75857-1

Overcoming Depression For Dummies
978-0-470-69430-5

Positive Psychology For Dummies
978-0-470-72136-0

PRINCE2 For Dummies, 2009 Edition
978-0-470-71025-8

Project Management For Dummies
978-0-470-71119-4

Psychometric Tests For Dummies
978-0-470-75366-8

Renting Out Your Property For Dummies, 3rd Edition
978-1-119-97640-0

Rugby Union For Dummies, 3rd Edition
978-1-119-99092-5

Sage One For Dummies
978-1-119-95236-7

Self-Hypnosis For Dummies
978-0-470-66073-7

Storing and Preserving Garden Produce For Dummies
978-1-119-95156-8

Study Skills For Dummies
978-0-470-74047-7

Teaching English as a Foreign Language For Dummies
978-0-470-74576-2

Time Management For Dummies
978-0-470-77765-7

Training Your Brain For Dummies
978-0-470-97449-0

Work-Life Balance For Dummies
978-0-470-71380-8

Writing a Dissertation For Dummies
978-0-470-74270-9

FOR DUMMIES®

Making Everything Easier!™

LANGUAGES

Spanish
FOR DUMMIES

978-0-470-68815-1
UK Edition

French
FOR DUMMIES

978-1-118-00464-7

Polish
FOR DUMMIES

978-1-119-97959-3
UK Edition

MUSIC

Ukulele
FOR DUMMIES

978-0-470-97799-6
UK Edition

Guitar Chords
FOR DUMMIES

978-0-470-66603-6
Lay-flat, UK Edition

DJing
FOR DUMMIES

978-0-470-66372-1
UK Edition

SCIENCE AND MATHS

Biology
FOR DUMMIES

978-0-470-59875-7

Algebra I
FOR DUMMIES

978-0-470-55964-2

Genetics
FOR DUMMIES

978-0-470-55174-5

Art For Dummies
978-0-7645-5104-8

Bass Guitar For Dummies, 2nd Edition
978-0-470-53961-3

Criminology For Dummies
978-0-470-39696-4

Currency Trading For Dummies, 2nd Edition
978-0-470-01851-4

Drawing For Dummies, 2nd Edition
978-0-470-61842-4

Forensics For Dummies
978-0-7645-5580-0

German For Dummies
978-0-470-90101-4

Guitar For Dummies, 2nd Edition
978-0-7645-9904-0

Hinduism For Dummies
978-0-470-87858-3

Index Investing For Dummies
978-0-470-29406-2

Knitting For Dummies, 2nd Edition
978-0-470-28747-7

Music Theory For Dummies, 2nd Edition
978-1-118-09550-8

Piano For Dummies, 2nd Edition
978-0-470-49644-2

Physics For Dummies, 2nd Edition
978-0-470-90324-7

Schizophrenia For Dummies
978-0-470-25927-6

Sex For Dummies, 3rd Edition
978-0-470-04523-7

Solar Power Your Home For Dummies, 2nd Edition
978-0-470-59678-4

The Titanic For Dummies
978-1-118-17766-2

Available wherever books are sold. For more information or to order direct go to
www.wiley.com or call +44 (0) 1243 843291